# 7 BASIC WEALTH STRATEGIES

For a More Rewarding and Fulfilling Life

WRITTEN BY
## VICTOR IDOKO
CFA, M. Comm (Finance), ADFP

CFV Services
Level 45, 680 George Street
Sydney NSW Australia

admin@cfvservices.com.au
cfvservices.com.au

**ISBN: 978-1-7637187-2-2**

**Printed in the Country purchased**

**First Edition: October, 2024**

## Acknowledgements

This book would not have been possible without the encouragement, support, and expertise of many people. I would like to extend my deepest gratitude to my team members for their endless effort to ensure the ship is still moving while I focussed and powered through this in a short period of time. For my family and friends for their endless patience and understanding during the countless hours I spent writing. A special thanks to my clients who were all so thrilled when they heard I was doing something like this and provided support.

I am also grateful to the financial professionals, coaches and mentors who shared their knowledge and experiences, helping to shape the contents of this book.

To my mother, whose unwavering support, encouragement, leadership by example and love have been my greatest source of inspiration and motivation. My usual saying is, 'my mother didn't work this hard for me to be average'. So I strive for the best I can be.

To my older sister, who was the first person to ever tell me to write a book. It only took me about 10 years to do it.

To my family, friends, who believed in me even when I thought twice about writing, and to all the readers embarking on their financial journeys – this book is for you.

# CONTENTS

# Foreword

We often view wealth as the ultimate achievement—the benchmark of success and happiness. Yet, from my years in business advisory, I've learned that true fulfilment isn't solely about financial gain. It's about creating a life that harmoniously balances financial security, personal well-being, and meaningful relationships.

Victor Idoko's 7 Basic Wealth Strategies: For a More Rewarding and Fulfilling Life offers a refreshing perspective on what it means to be truly wealthy. This book goes beyond traditional financial advice to present a holistic approach to wealth. Victor's insights simplify complex financial concepts, making them practical and actionable for everyone, regardless of where they are on their journey.

What I find most compelling about Victor's approach is his emphasis on blending wealth with health and relationships. He understands that financial success is just one piece of a larger puzzle. By addressing these integrated aspects of life, he provides a guide that not only helps you build wealth but also enhances your overall quality of life.

Victor's wisdom comes from a blend of real-world experience and a genuine passion for helping others succeed. As you dive into this book, you'll discover practical strategies you can start applying right away. More importantly, you'll gain a fresh perspective on how to use your financial success as a tool for a richer, more fulfilling life.

It's a privilege to introduce you to Victor Idoko and his insightful work. This book is more than just a financial guide—it's a roadmap to a life where your wealth enhances everything that truly matters. Embrace these strategies, and you'll find that true wealth is about living a life that is both rewarding and meaningful.

Victor's a beast!

Sincerely,

**Philip Khao Virtual CFO**
**Director of Solve Accounting**

**https://solveaccounting.com.au/about-us/philip-khao/**

# Preface

Welcome to 7 Basic Wealth Strategies: For a More Rewarding and Fulfilling Life, your guide to financial and investment planning. This book stems from my passion for helping individuals achieve financial independence and security. It also arises from my frustration with traditional money books that often focus narrowly on property or shares, without providing a holistic view of financial planning and the essential strategies one must employ.

As a financial planner, I've seen the transformative power of smart financial decisions, but I've also witnessed the confusion and anxiety that often accompany financial planning. I believe it's crucial for financial planners to be more vocal about what people should do, the risks of taking action or inaction, and the opportunity costs involved. Doing nothing or doing the wrong thing can have significant consequences, just as staying the course can yield substantial rewards.

My goal in writing this book is to present simple, actionable steps that anyone can take to improve their financial situation. But beyond finances, I emphasise that true fulfilment in life comes from a balance of health, wealth, and relationships. Whether you're just beginning your financial journey or seeking to refine your strategy, this book offers insights and tools to help you make informed decisions.

You can expect clear explanations of financial concepts, step-by-step guides to various strategies, and real-life examples to illustrate key points. By the end of this book, I hope you will feel more confident in managing your finances and achieving your goals.

I also aspire for financial advice to become accessible and affordable for everyone. While this is not yet the case, I aim to take a step in the right direction with this book. Thank you for joining me on this journey toward financial empowerment and a more rewarding life.

## General Advice Warning

The content provided in this book is for general informational purposes only and does not constitute personal financial advice. While I am a qualified and experienced financial professional, any advice included here has been prepared without taking into account your individual objectives, financial situation, or specific needs. It is crucial that you assess your own circumstances before acting on any information presented in this book.

Before making any financial decisions or investments, I strongly recommend you consult with a financial adviser who can take into account your unique circumstances and provide tailored advice. Additionally, ensure that you review the relevant Product Disclosure Statement (PDS) and Target Market Determination (TMD) before making any decisions about the products discussed here. These documents are vital in helping you understand the product's features, risks, and suitability for your situation.

As a professional in this field, I take my responsibility to provide sound advice very seriously. However, the strategies and ideas discussed in this book may not be right for everyone.

Financial planning is highly personal, and while my goal is to equip you with valuable knowledge and insights, it's essential to seek professional guidance tailored to your specific needs.

Your financial well-being is important, so please take the time to ensure that any actions you take are well-suited to your goals and situation.

# CHAPTER 1
## START WITH THE END IN MIND

# STRATEGY 1 – HAVE A PLAN

## What would you like to achieve?

### What would you like life to look like in 10 years? Write it down!

When you are trying to navigate to a destination, you need to know the most efficient way to get there. If you don't know where you are going, you will end up nowhere. Just like in wealth building and finances, if you don't have a wealth goal for your rewarding and fulfilling life in mind, you will just go wherever the wind takes you.

So, even before you read this book any further, take time to think about and write down your goal. Writing it down works wonders as you will understand your goal on different levels. You will think about it more, and most of all, you will also be more sure of the goal.

At minimum, write down what you want for yourself and if you have family, what you want for all of you in the next 10 years. Even better, create a 10 year vision board! There is ample space at the end of this chapter with prompts for this to be written down but still use the space below to write down your thoughts.

# The Importance of 10-Year Goals

Setting 10-year goals is a critical component of long-term planning and personal development. Your goals provide a clear vision of where you want to be in the future, guiding your decisions and actions in the present.

## 1. Vision and Direction

### Long-Term Perspective:

- **Clarity:** 10-year goals help you see the bigger picture, providing a sense of direction and purpose. They allow you to envision your future clearly and set a roadmap to achieve it.

- **Motivation:** Knowing where you want to be in 10 years can be highly motivating. It keeps you focused on the end goal, especially during challenging times.

**Example:** If your 10-year goal is to own a successful business, this vision will drive your daily efforts and decisions, keeping you motivated to overcome obstacles.

## 2. Strategic Planning

### Breaking Down Goals:

- **Milestones:** A 10-year goal can be broken down into smaller, more manageable milestones, making the goal seem less overwhelming and more achievable.

- **Action Steps:** These milestones can be further divided into actionable steps, providing a clear plan of what needs to be done.

**Example:** To achieve a 10-year goal of financial independence, you might set milestones like saving a certain amount each year, investing in various assets, and reducing debt.

## 3. Personal Growth

**Continuous Improvement:**

- **Skill Development:** Long-term goals often require you to acquire new skills and knowledge. This commitment to learning fosters continuous personal growth.

- **Adaptability:** Working towards long-term goals helps you develop resilience and adaptability, as you learn to navigate and adjust to changes and challenges over time.

**Example:** If your 10-year goal is to become more patient and reduce anger, you can practice mindfulness, seek therapy, and engage in stress-relief activities to ensure you develop a calmer and more composed demeanour.

## 4. Financial Planning

**Building Wealth:**

- **Investment Strategy:** A 10-year goal provides a time horizon for financial planning, allowing you to develop and implement a sound, SMART investment strategy. This helps put less pressure on yourself now but with consistency all the small efforts add up to a larger and amazing outcome.

- **Savings and Budgeting:** Long-term financial goals encourage disciplined saving and budgeting habits, which are crucial for achieving financial stability and growth.

**Example:** If your 10-year goal is to buy a house, you can plan your savings, investments, and budget to ensure you have the necessary funds when the time comes.

## 5. Career Advancement

**Professional Development:**

- **Career Path:** Setting long-term career goals helps you map out a clear career path. It guides your educational choices, job changes, and professional development activities.

- **Networking:** Long-term goals often require building a strong professional network. This network can provide support, opportunities, and mentorship.

**Example:** If your 10-year goal is to become a top executive in your industry, you will need to continuously improve your leadership skills, industry knowledge, and professional network.

## 6. Life Balance

### Wealth, Health and Relationship Harmony:

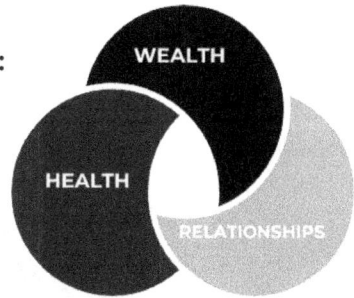

- **Prioritisation:** Long-term goals help you prioritise what is most important in your life, balancing professional ambitions with personal aspirations. This is essential for achieving harmony among wealth, health, and relationships.

  - **Wealth:** There are times when focusing on wealth is necessary to build a foundation for a better future. A 10-year plan makes it clear when to prioritise financial growth, ensuring that you have the resources to support your relationships and health in the long run.

  - **Health:** Prioritising health is crucial for sustaining your ability to work towards your long-term goals. A balanced plan ensures that you allocate time for physical activity, healthy eating, and mental well-being, recognising that good health is the cornerstone of sustained productivity and happiness.

  - **Relationships:** Planning for the long term encourages you to consider the impact of your goals on your family, relationships, and hobbies, fostering a balanced and fulfilling life. Relationships are a vast and complex area, encompassing not just people but also with inanimate objects and personal interests. Your relationship with your phone, for example, can significantly impact your progress towards your long-term goals. Assess whether spending time in front of screens aligns with your aspirations. If these activities support your goals, they can be considered healthy. If not, it may be time to reassess and adjust your habits. Similarly, cultivating a good relationship with your hobbies is essential as they provide joy, relaxation, and personal growth, contributing to your overall well-being.

**Example:** If your 10-year goal is to maintain a great wealth, health, and relationship balance, you can plan your career moves and personal life to ensure you have time for your health, family, hobbies, and self-care.

Setting 10-year goals is essential for providing vision and direction, enabling strategic planning, fostering personal growth, advancing your career, and maintaining life balance. These goals are your guiding star, helping you navigate the complexities of life with purpose and determination. By breaking them down into actionable steps and staying committed to your vision, you can achieve remarkable progress and fulfilment over the next decade.

> **'Visualise and draw the plans of the house before you lay the foundation'.**

**Answering the following questions will allow you get to the 10-year (2035) goal easily.**

**Income Goal:** "How much weekly income do you want in your pocket after taxes?"

**Example:** "$2,220 each a week for me and my partner." Don't forget this is adjusted with inflation, so this is actually an amount that is equivalent to $1,500 in today's dollars. Roughly 1.48 (4% growth every year) multiplied by the current amount you earn or what you want to earn.

**Work Schedule:** "What is your ideal work schedule?"

**Example:** "4 days a week, 8 hours a day."

**Weekend Activities:** "How do you envision spending your weekends?"

**Example:** "Family activities and quality time with my partner and loved ones every other weekend."

**Property Goal:** "What kind of home would you like to live in?"

**Example:** "A 3-bedroom house in a suburb like Rockdale Sydney with 50% of the mortgage paid off."

**Passive Income:** "What amount of passive income are you aiming for?"

**Example:** "$5,000 a month net of investment costs." At a cash rate plus 5% (roughly currently 10%) earnings rate you are looking at about 600k invested.

**Lifestyle:** "Describe your desired lifestyle."

**Example:** "One day off weekly for personal time, traveling with family for 2 weeks overseas and 1 week locally each year."

**Fitness Level:** "What fitness level do you want to maintain?"

**Example:** "Running 5 km and working out 2 times a week."

**Additional Goals:** "Are there any other goals you'd like to achieve?"

**Example:** "Donating $5,000 annually to charities, learning another language, and focusing on health and relationships."

A heuristic you can use if you are still not sure or you are really pleased with where you are right now is to multiply all your investments earnings and income by 1.48 to get to what it should be in 10 years. This way you don't move backwards and maintain the current living standards you have.

# CHAPTER 2
# KNOW YOUR BIASES

# STRATEGY 2 –
# UNDERSTAND YOURSELF AND WHAT
# MAY BE HOLDING YOU BACK

## Introduction to Financial Biases

As a financial planner, the more I can understand my client, the better I can provide tailored value to them. I try to understand each client's biases. We all have a few, so finding ways to help them understand and mitigate or eliminate these biases is powerful for financial success.

Financial biases are the sneaky mental traps that can lead us astray in managing our money. They stem from our psychological predispositions and can have a profound impact on our financial decisions. Understanding these biases is the first step toward smarter, more rational financial planning and investment steps. Biases can be generally classified into emotional and cognitive biases (according to the CFA institution which really helped me understand this for myself and for my clients).

Cognitive biases typically stem from a lack of understanding or faulty reasoning. You can eliminate cognitive biases through education, better information, and training in critical thinking. For example, learning about common cognitive biases like anchoring or overconfidence and using structured decision-making frameworks can help you make more rational decisions.

Emotional biases, on the other hand, need to be mitigated rather than eliminated because they are deeply rooted in our psychology and emotions. These biases, such as loss aversion and status quo bias, are harder to overcome entirely because they are tied to our feelings and instincts. Strategies to mitigate their impact include increasing self-awareness, practicing emotional regulation techniques like mindfulness, and seeking objective advice from third parties. By recognising and managing emotional biases, individuals can make more balanced decisions.

Below is a list of a few of the biases that affect people with their finances and investments that I have come across a lot, and how you can notice and eliminate them.

## Mental Accounting: The Sneaky Saboteur

Mental accounting is when you treat money differently based on its source or intended use. Think of it as your brain playing tricks on you, making that bonus feel like "fun money" while your salary is for "serious stuff."

**Real-Life Example:** You get a tax refund and think, "Hello, new gadget!" Meanwhile, your credit card debt is laughing in the corner. Integrate that refund into your overall strategy and make smart moves, not impulse buys.

**Questions to See if I Display this Bias:**

**Wealth:** How am I treating different sources of income differently, and how might that be affecting my overall financial strategy?

**Health:** In what ways am I allocating my health expenses differently based on where the money comes from? Do I even consciously allocate any funds to my health?

**Relationships:** How do I decide where to spend money on my relationships, and am I neglecting important areas because of this?

### How to Beat it:

- **Unified Budget:** Forget separate piggy banks. Use a comprehensive budget/spending plan that aligns with your financial goals, no matter where the money comes from. Follow the process in the next chapter for all your sources of income.

- **Stay Alert:** Be aware of this trickery. Treat all money with the same respect, whether it's from your paycheck or the bank of mum and dad.

This is a cognitive bias, which can be eliminated as soon as you understand what you are doing and follow the above steps.

## Status Quo Bias: The Comfort Zone Con

This is your inner sloth, loving the current state of affairs and resisting change even when it's obviously better on the other side. This is an emotional bias and has to be mitigated. It can always be better on the other side but it is a diminishing return, so it is important to know that, as long as you are taking steps you are doing the right thing, even if you are not in the best state of affairs yet.

**Real-Life Example:** You're clinging to that high-interest mortgage like it's a family heirloom, even though refinancing could save you big bucks. Time to make the switch and laugh all the way to the bank.

**Questions to See if I Display this Bias:**

**Wealth:** What financial decisions am I avoiding because they disrupt my current comfort, and how could changing them benefit me?

**Health:** What health routines am I sticking to just because they are familiar, and how could exploring new options improve my well-being?

**Relationships:** How might my relationships benefit from changes I've been hesitant to make, and what steps can I take to initiate those changes?

**How to Beat It:**

- **Cost-Benefit Analysis:** Regularly weigh the pros and cons of sticking with your current financial decisions versus making a change. This can be hard to do without any help from an Accountability police/ partner but it is possible.

- **Baby Steps:** Make gradual changes. Dip your toes in the water before diving in. From only doing something about it for 5 mins a day to an hour, you will have made significant changes in no time and built an amazing habit.

# Endowment Bias: The Over-Valuation Overlord (Sometimes Under-Valuation)

You think your stuff is worth more just because it's yours. Very cute, but not practical. This translates into several facets in life, be it your health, wealth or relationships. This can also work in the opposite as well, where you value something less because you have it. This is an emotional bias and can only be mitigated, very hard to eliminate but worth a ton to be aware of it.

**Real-Life Example:** You're trying to sell your house for way more than it's worth because you've got "memories." Buyers don't care about your memories. Price it right and move on. You cannot time the market, as long as the reason for selling is logical, the market should give you a price.

**Questions to Ask:**

**Wealth:** How am I valuing my assets based on personal attachment rather than market value, and what impact does this have on my financial decisions?

**Health:** In what ways might I be overestimating my fitness level or health status because of my attachment to my current routine?

**Relationships:** How do my personal attachments influence my perception of my relationships, and what can I do to assess them more objectively?

_____

_____

_____

**How to Beat it:**

- **Objective Valuation:** Get third-party appraisals or compare market values. Please don't compare market value for something like your partner (relationships) or your running splits times (health) - those are very specific to you but there can still be a bias in there.

- **Detach Emotionally:** Your possessions aren't precious or worthless just because they're yours.

## Overconfidence Bias: The Cocky Contender

You think you're a financial genius.
Spoiler: You're not.

Overconfidence is the tendency for individuals to overestimate their own abilities, knowledge, or predictions. This cognitive bias can lead people to believe they are more capable than they actually are, particularly in areas where they lack expertise. In the context of finance and investments, overconfidence can result in risky decision-making and underestimation of potential pitfalls.

**Real-Life Example:** You're betting big on a stock because you "just know" it's going to skyrocket. When it tanks, you're left holding the bag. Diversify and listen to the experts. Even if it doesn't tank, if you haven't done a detailed analysis and been doing this for a while, you were just a lucky Lance.

## Questions to Ask:

**Wealth:** How am I overestimating my financial knowledge or investment skills, and what steps can I take to make more informed decisions?

**Health:** In what areas of my health am I overly confident, and how can I seek out more accurate assessments?

**Relationships:** How might my overconfidence in understanding my partner's needs be affecting our relationship, and what can I do to improve communication?

## How to Beat it:

- **Seek Feedback:** Get second opinions to keep your ego in check.
- **Data-Driven Decisions:** Trust the numbers, not your gut. Expert intuition (the rapid, seemingly instinctual understanding or decision-making ability that is developed through extensive experience and deep knowledge in a particular field) can come with time - decades or full time service to a profession.

## Anchoring Bias: The First Impression Fiasco

It anchors you down.

Anchoring bias is the cognitive bias where an individual relies too heavily on an initial piece of information (the "anchor") when making decisions. This initial information serves as a reference point and influences subsequent judgments and decisions, even if it is irrelevant or misleading. It is a cognitive bias, so easy to overcome once you know it is there.

**Real-Life Example:** The first price you hear during salary negotiations becomes your anchor, even if it's low. Push past it and aim higher. You're worth it.

The price you set on selling a stock or house, even though the market might have significantly changed over time.

**Questions to Ask:**

**Wealth:** How are my financial decisions being influenced by initial information, and how can I gather more data to make better choices?

**Health:** How is my fitness plan or diet influenced by the first advice I received, and what other options should I consider?

**Relationships:** How have my first impressions of people influenced my relationships, and what can I do to reassess them more fairly?

**How to Beat it:**

- **Gather More Info:** Don't let the first thing you hear set the tone. Get multiple opinions.

- **Adjust and Adapt:** Be flexible and open to new information. Always ask why do I want that price for this asset?

## Loss Aversion: The Fear Factor

Loss aversion is an emotional bias that describes why the pain of losing is psychologically more powerful than the pleasure of gaining. Essentially, people prefer to avoid losses rather than acquiring equivalent gains; losing $100 feels more painful than the joy of gaining $100.

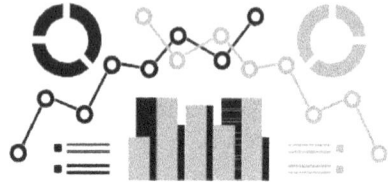

**Real-Life Example:** You're holding onto a tanking stock to avoid admitting defeat. Dump it and move on. There's more fish in the sea, or rather, more stocks in the market. This is very important in times of crisis or where all stocks are falling but some have fallen more than others with no obvious reason, you can sell the stock that has fallen to buy the stock that has fallen more for an increased future gain.

**Question to Ask:**

**Wealth:** Am I holding onto investments to avoid losses, and what might be the benefits of letting them go?

**Health:** How is my fear of losing progress affecting my willingness to change my health routine, and what could I gain from making changes?

**Relationships:** How is my fear of ending a relationship impacting my well-being, and what steps can I take to address this?

**How to Beat it:**

- **Balanced Risk:** Weigh both risks and rewards before making decisions.

- **Focus on the Long-Term:** Think about where you want to be, not just what you might lose today.

## Herd Mentality: The Sheep Syndrome

You follow the crowd, often into a terrible decision. Baaad move.

Herd mentality, also known as herd behaviour, is the tendency for individuals to follow the actions and behaviours of a larger group, often disregarding their own analysis or intuition. This bias leads people to make decisions based on what others are doing rather than on their own independent evaluation. This is a cognitive bias, as it often involves lack of knowledge on what to do, so we follow Mr. and Mrs. Jones down the road.

**Real-Life Examples in Finance:**

**Stock Market Bubbles:**
Example: During the dot-com bubble of the late 1990s, many investors bought technology stocks because everyone else was, leading to inflated prices. When the bubble burst, those who followed the herd faced significant losses.

**Cryptocurrency Mania:**
Example: The rapid rise of Bitcoin and other cryptocurrencies saw many investors jumping in because others were making money. This herd behaviour drove prices up, but when the market corrected, many latecomers suffered substantial losses.

**Question to Ask:**

**Wealth:** How are my investment decisions being influenced by what others are doing, and how can I base my decisions on my own research?

**Health:** How is my fitness regimen influenced by popular trends, and what might be a better approach for me personally?

**Relationships:** How are social pressures affecting my relationship choices, and how can I make more independent decisions?

**How to Beat it:**

- **Do Your Research:** Make decisions based on your analysis, not the crowd's. The crowds are usually right in social norms, they are usually wrong in the next hot investment.

- **Critical Thinking:** Question the herd. Be the black sheep in a sea of white.

# Confirmation Bias: The Echo Chamber Effect

You only listen to what you already believe, ignoring the rest. Comforting, but dangerous.

Confirmation bias is the tendency to search for, interpret, and remember information that confirms one's preconceptions while ignoring or discounting contradictory evidence. This cognitive bias can lead to overconfidence in one's beliefs and poor decision-making.

**Real-Life Examples:**

**Investment Decisions:**
**Example:** An investor strongly believes in the potential of a particular industry, such as renewable energy. They seek out positive news and reports about the industry while ignoring warning signs or negative analyses. This could lead to an over-concentration of investments in that sector and increased risk.

**Economic Forecasting:**
**Example:** An 'economist' (yours truly) predicts a market downturn and only pays attention to data that supports this view, ignoring signs of economic growth or stability. This confirmation bias can lead to skewed forecasts and poor strategic decisions.

**Questions to Ask:**

**Wealth:** How am I seeking out information that confirms my existing financial beliefs, and what steps can I take to consider alternative viewpoints?

**Health:** How might my current health practices be influenced by only looking for evidence that supports them, and how can I challenge myself to explore new methods?

**Relationships:** How do my interactions with others reinforce my existing beliefs about relationships, and what can I do to be more open to different perspectives?

**How to Beat it:**

- **Seek Diverse Opinions:** Listen to different perspectives, even if they challenge your views.
- **Self-Questioning:** Regularly reassess your beliefs. Don't get too cosy.

## Conclusion:

### Embracing Awareness and Building Good Habits

Understanding and recognising these biases is the first step towards making more informed and rational decisions in all aspects of life—whether it's managing your wealth, improving your health, or nurturing your relationships. While some biases can be eliminated through education and awareness, others require ongoing awareness and mitigation.

Remember, progress starts with small, consistent actions. By being mindful of these biases, you can begin to develop habits that lead to better decision-making. Don't be discouraged by the complexity of these concepts; instead, focus on taking baby steps in the right direction. Gradually, these steps will compound into significant positive changes, helping you achieve your long-term goals and leading to a more balanced and fulfilling life.

Stay curious, keep learning, and continually strive to improve. Your journey towards better decision-making is a lifelong process, but with awareness and dedication, you can navigate it successfully. Here's to embracing awareness, building good habits, and making smart decisions that pave the way for a prosperous future.

# CHAPTER 3
## CASH FLOW

# STRATEGY 3 –
# KNOW YOUR NUMBERS AND WHAT YOU SPEND

## Personal Cash Flow

Cash flow is the most important foundation to building wealth and reducing the stress that comes with finances. If you have enough of this and have planned properly, things just work a lot easier. One of the major mistakes people make with cash flow is having too many buckets/wallets that you allocate money to. This causes you to move funds around too much and lose momentum with money management. On the personal side, if you have more than 4-5 buckets it starts to be inefficient. You can have multiple items linked to one bucket. For personal finances the buckets are:

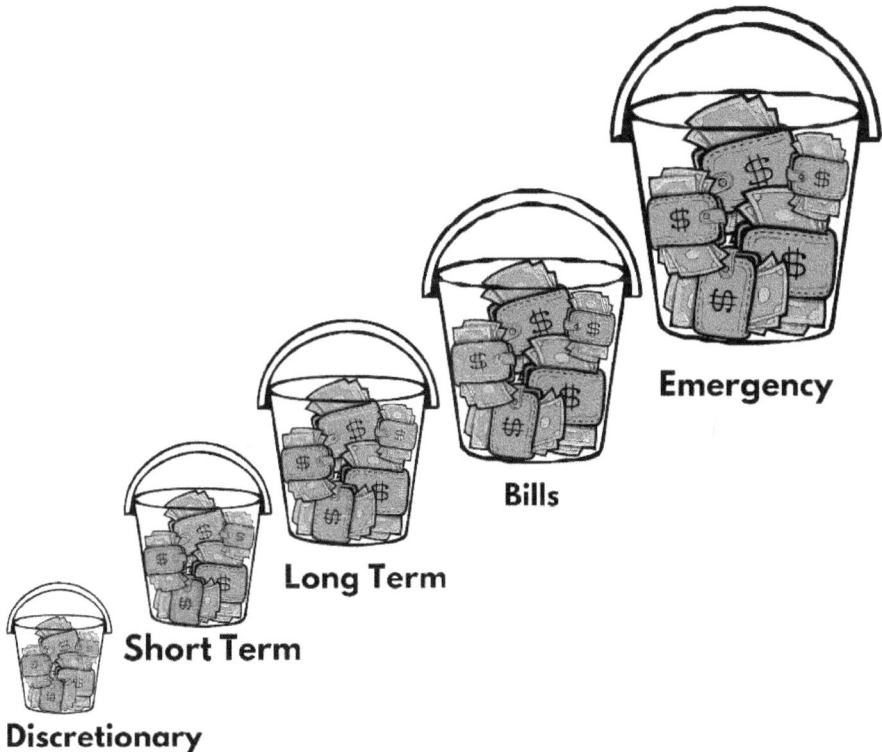

Emergency

Bills

Long Term

Short Term

Discretionary

# Why Should You Use Percentages for Saving?

Using percentages for a spending plan instead of actual amounts offers key benefits:

## 1. Scalability:

- **Adapts to Income and Expense Changes:** Whether your income/expenses increases or decreases, percentages ensure your budget remains proportional.

## 2. Financial Discipline:

- **Consistent Savings and Spending:** Percentages help prioritise expenses, ensuring essential categories like savings and necessities are consistently funded.

## 3. Consistency:

- **Maintains Financial Habits:** Ensures balanced spending and saving habits, preventing overspending.

## 4. Goal Alignment:

- **Supports Financial Goals:** Percentages can be aligned with long-term goals, ensuring continuous progress.

## 5. Adaptability:

- **Responsive to Life Changes:** Adapts easily to life events such as job changes or economic shifts.

## 6. Financial Awareness:

- **Promotes Understanding:** Helps you understand spending patterns and make informed financial decisions.

  Using percentages for budgeting ensures your financial plan remains adaptable, disciplined, and aligned with your goals, providing a stable framework for managing your finances effectively.

**Explanation of Each Bucket (Personal):**

- **Bills -** This is the bucket where you would potentially spend the most. Everything you need to survive, that you usually do, that you want to do, and that consistently comes up in your life will fall into this bucket.

A few examples are: groceries, dining out with friends and family, family items, baby items, energy bills, rent or mortgage, health and fitness, and clothes. If you fit all these usual items within 60% of your disposable (after tax income), you are doing very well.

- **Short/medium term:** These are the items that we can refer to as planned but you can survive without if you end up not saving enough for. These are items like travel, furniture, gifts to loved ones, a new car, wedding celebrations, and so on. This account should be consistently growing for a young family to ensure you are in a good position and not worried about money. For single people who want families, it is crucial to keep this account growing for a time when cash flow might not be as substantial when kids come into the picture. Usually the family income drops for a period of time and you need to have enough buffer for this. If you can consistently put 20% of your disposable income into this bucket, you are doing well. It should be growing by at least 5% every year before children. If you already have children or you are not planning for them, this bucket doesn't need to grow over time.

- **Discretionary:** This is the fun account. I always say your spending plan and money management is a lifestyle, so enjoy it along the way. This is the bucket that you can really enjoy. This is the bucket that allows you to spend on anything you want. If you are a couple, and you tend to want to spend on separate fun stuff, you should definitely use separate accounts for this and each partner can spend on what they want. This bucket should have 10% of your disposable income.

- **Long term:** This is the long term bucket for your wealth creation. Your long term bucket is a passive investment bucket that will create wealth to replace your income in 15 - 25 years depending on your timeframe and family situation. If you aren't planning to have kids, you could do this in as little as 15 years. You should be putting at least 10% to this bucket consistently to ensure you have a rewarding life. This allocated amount can be used to pay off an investment mortgage or put into a diversified portfolio of stocks. We will explore this further under the investment section.

  - There are a couple of different options for your investment returns:
    - Keep reinvesting it into the chosen investment, or
    - Distribute it into your buckets with the percentages I spoke about above.

  - What you will find after doing this for a while is your accounts will start to grow and you get into an effortless cycle of growing wealth.

  - The idea is over the long term and when you reach the wealth preservation stage, you will no longer need to put money aside for long term investments.

  My philosophy is you have to enjoy your hard earned money and build wealth how you like. For some, it will be putting money aside for the kids or just spending it on yourself if you don't have kids. However you want to do it, following these percentage rules will help you make sure your financial life is running sustainably.

- You might be thinking, where are the emergency funds? Yes, you should also have this bucket ('5th bucket'). I don't really call this a bucket as it can be directly put into your mortgage, if you have a redraw facility (ability to take the money out when you need it) or a bank account not linked to your 'cash flow'. You should have 3 to 6 months of your salary because of the following:

  - Let's assume you had to leave your job, how long will it take you to find a new one?

  - How comfortable do you feel about not having available cash? This is a feeling (a bias) so going past 6 months starts to do you harm. This is because the money should be working hard for you and not just lying around.

- Do you have a run-down car or house? If you do, you want to build this emergency account up higher for any big emergencies that come up.

- Are you a full timer, contractor or business owner? The full timer needs less savings than a new business owner.

- Do you think you might need to provide for someone who will be dependent on you in the near future? Old parents or unruly relatives you can't help but help.

# Tips for Personal Cash Flow and Spending Plans

## 1. Name the Accounts

Your short term accounts can be called 'Travel' for instance. There is an emotional connection when you name your accounts, you stick with the goal longer. Here are some amazing discretionary account names I like.

| The Dream Fund | Treat Yo' Self Account | Splurge Stash | YOLO Yields |
|---|---|---|---|
| Happy Wallet | Retail Therapy Reserve | Goodies Galore | Fun Fund |
| Bliss Bucks | Bucket List Bank | Joy Jar | Spend-it Savings |
| Pamper Pouch | Indulgence Income | Cheerful Chest | Impulse Investment |
| Giggle Gold | Wishful Wallet | Adventure Account | Luxury Loot |

Table 3.1 - Fun names for Discretionary accounts

## 2. Automate the Transfer to Go in Each Pay Period

If you get paid weekly, let the payments automatically transfer a day after your pay. This helps with you sticking to the plan and works wonders as people adapt to situations they are put in, so you are ensuring you do the same with your spending plan.

### 3. Don't Go From Zero to Hero

If you are not used to saving anything, start with just a small amount - say 2% (2% of the average weekly wage is $28). This is an okay start. When I got my first job in 2013, I was putting $10 a fortnight into my investment account. The behaviour is more important than the amount in the early stages, and no amount is too small to start with.

### 4. Hide the Accounts

Looking at your accounts everyday will not make them work fast or harder. Once this is all set up, you want minimal visibility of these accounts. The only accounts you want to constantly look at are your bills and 'goodies galore' accounts. For the rest, you want to be pleasantly surprised at the end of a year or more as to what has been put away for your future self.

### 5. If You Fall Off, Get Right Back On

I have fallen off my spending plan lots of times and it only pays to get back on and ensure you stay longer than the last time you fell off. Before you know it, you are sticking to your plan for years.

### 6. Allocate Windfalls the Same Way

When you get tax back, bonuses from work, a gift of a small amount, allocate it the same way as your regular income. If you want to be aggressive with your wealth creation, you can allocate more to the long term and short term. I encourage you to always put something in the 'happy wallet' as well.

### 7. Get an Accountability Mate

One person that you can share your finances with and potentially have a similar hobby or two can keep you both accountable. This will only take about 10 mins max. Don't ask someone that you know will not help the process, we all have the one mate who won't help but are in the fun category of mates. This is important, so build something you will truly enjoy with someone who will push you in the right direction.

# Business Cash Flow

Only about 50% of businesses make it past their 5th year anniversary. While there are many reasons a business will fail, one is financial management. Financial management is broken down into several aspects like cash flow management, capital management, risk management, and tax management. The aspect I will focus on is cash flow allocation under cash flow management.

This is important as cash is King and when done properly it can really help you make great decisions about other aspects of your business. When done early, it can help you stay in business and thrive. Just like personal cash flow, you can use the bucket system to ensure you have funds in each bucket.

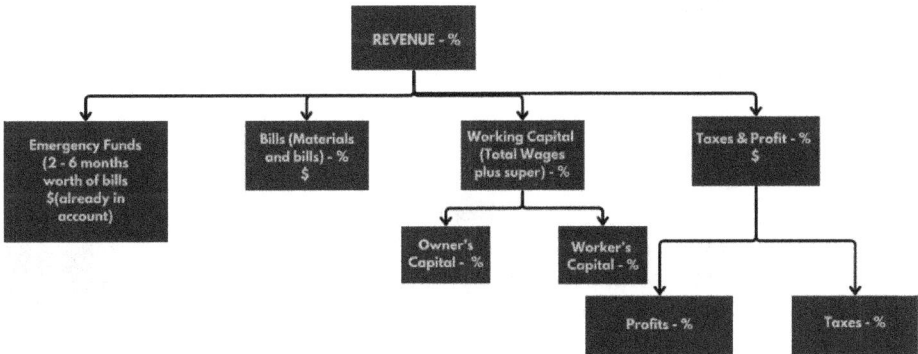

BUSINESS - pw, pf or pm
ACCOUNTS

**Explanation of each bucket:**

- **Bills/Materials** - As soon as a business starts, you will have some ongoing costs to keep the lights on. This makes it difficult if you are not already receiving revenue. You want to go into a business with a clear understanding of how long before revenue starts coming in, so you can plan appropriately. As soon as revenue starts coming in, you want to put away a percentage for your bills (and materials - depending on your type of business).

For a construction company providing services, you might be spending 30% to 50% on bills and materials. The costs have a range because there can be running a poor business or paying for materials needed. Assuming materials are paid by their client, you should be spending only about 30% on bills. This percentage has to include everything else, like payments of operations and fees for subscriptions. Think about accounting bills, insurance, office supplies, rent/mortgage on commercial premises, utilities, legal, marketing, and so on.

- **Worker's and Owner's Capital** - This is everything related to paying a team member or contractor their wages, superannuation, GST, benefits, etc. It will probably be the largest ticket item. If you don't have team members, you may use contractors so you will need to budget appropriately for them as well. Using the example of Mr and Mrs Construction Pty Ltd, they would probably be spending 40% of revenue on this. If you don't have many contractors and do most of the work yourself, you will then just pay yourself the 40%. A business owner being able to pay themselves what they actually deserve in the first few months to years of running a business is rare. Be aware of this and always factor in the value you create in the business as a business owner - the value of the business itself. It is more valuable than what you pay yourself.

  However, you must set aside money you should be paying yourself. This is very important because if you want to bring in partners later on or just expand, the business should owe you a certain amount to compensate you for your effort.

  - To emphasise the fact of this, paying yourself as a business owner, I have taught this concept a lot and also learnt it from the book "Profit First". As a business owner, you are your most valuable team member because if you were not there, there would be no business and without a business there are no other team members.

  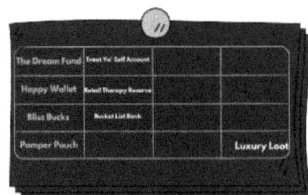

  - Compensating or recording your value fairly is also important because it ensures you have on record, at least, what the business owes you in the situation of a business purchase or involving other partners. This should not be just in your head but on file.

An example is, if you pay yourself at least 45k a year, this is less than the tax rate for a small business, so it is worth paying yourself to then just put this money back into the company (as a loan to the business from you) which provides you the capital to invest in the business but still ensures you don't pay more taxes if your business is making a profit.

You will have a $6,962 ($11,250 less $4,288) benefit if you are making a profit already. It is definitely not this straightforward, so speak to your accountant as needed and be guided by a finance professional that understands and deals with business owners. However, the benefit is when you put the money back into the business, it is on record that the business owes you $45,000 - $4,288 = $40,712. Yes, there are other obligations when you pay yourself a salary like super but if you are making a profit, it is in your best interest to put something, slowly, away for your retirement.

○ If you have any tax deductions in your personal name, some of this tax paid by the company is actually returned to you via this process. So a different way to see this is that you are taking money (tax paid by the business) from the business into your personal name/bank account in a tax efficient way. This can add up to tens of thousands of dollars over time.

- **Taxes** - Lots of business owners get run out of business when they find out their tax bill is massive and they have not kept money aside. At a bare minimum, you want to put 10% aside for the first 2 years. After that it really depends on how much profit you are making and this should drastically reduce in the next few years as the business grows. This percentage will help with GST payments and company tax payments. It is a complex area to prepare for but 10% until 2-5 years into the business is the bare minimum. Remember this is excluding PAYG tax as this should be part of the owners/workers capital account.

- **Profits** - This is the favourite account of business owners. It is your Luxury Loot (going back to table 3.1). This is the benefit you get out of running a business and it should have a clear purpose from the start. Profit for purpose can mean giving a certain percentage every year to a charity, growing the business, helping team members in need, whatever you want to do with it. Having a clear purpose around this helps you retain the funds in the account and even work harder and smarter to get to the dream goal. This margin should increase over time but it might not depending on the size of the business you want. At a bare minimum, if you are reading this and want to/are running a business, 10% should be your starting point. The reason I say this is because you are obviously looking for ways to grow and improve, so you can push yourself to start and grow from here.

Referring to the figure below with net profit margins in several industries, an easy way is to work backwards from what profit margin you want to have and then categorising this into the relevant buckets.

**Profit Margins Across Major Industries - Bar Chart**

Profit Margin

Max Profit Margin    Min Profit Margin

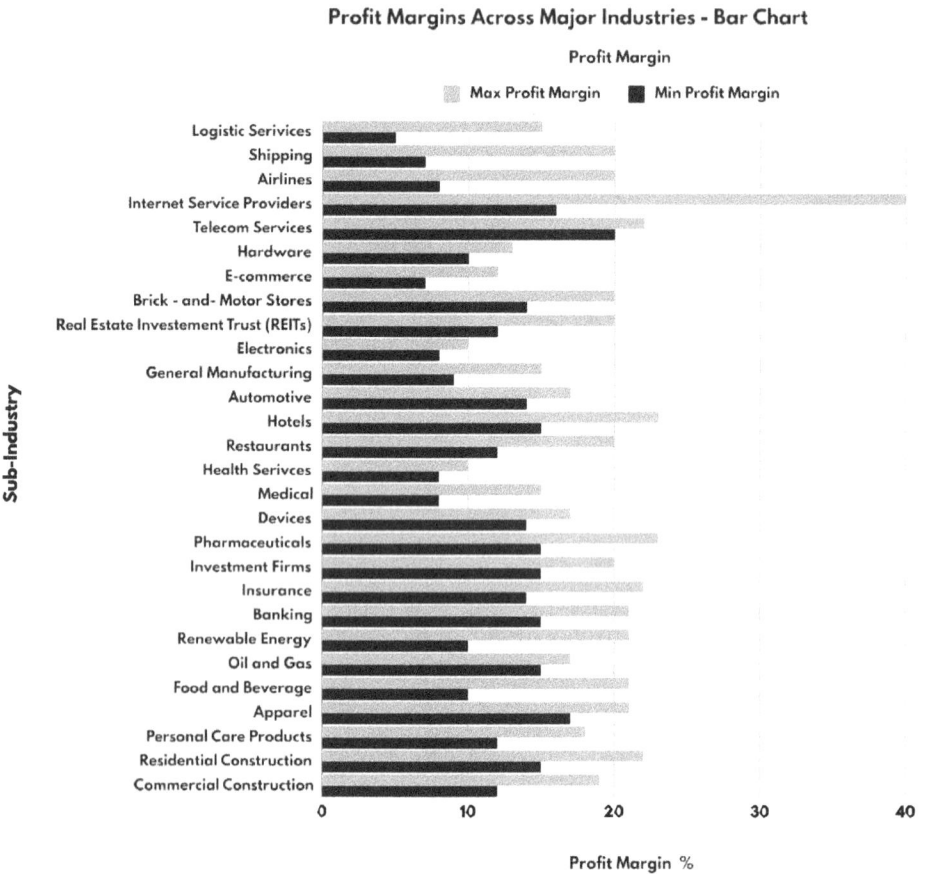

Sub-Industry

Profit Margin %

As your business grows, you will grow out of this model. Generally when a business starts turning over 2 million dollars or more, there will be different models to follow.

# CHAPTER 4

# THE ART AND SCIENCE OF INVESTING

# STRATEGY 4 –
# START INVESTING NOW, EVEN IF IT IS $10 A WEEK, DON'T STOP AND DON'T STOCK PICK, START NOW!

## Introduction

I was intrigued with investing once I got to understand it. It felt like magic to me, you put your money somewhere and it can do the heavy lifting for you. I remember my dad getting me to open cheques for him when I was 5 years old and wondering what they are. He explained someone is giving him money because he gave them money. I was stunned and didn't really understand the full concept then, but that is my first vivid memory of investing.

Investing is an art, a science, and most importantly, a behaviour that can be strengthened with education and experience. It's about making informed decisions, understanding the nuances of different asset classes, and strategically allocating resources to build wealth over time. As a financial planner, I firmly believe that the best investment you can make is in yourself—your human capital. However, over time, your human capital should be strategically converted into financial capital to secure your financial future.

## Types of Capital

### Human Capital: Your Greatest Asset

**Investing in Yourself.** Human capital refers to the economic value of your skills, knowledge, and experiences. It is the foundation upon which you build your career and generate income. Investing in your education, professional development, and health can yield substantial returns in the form of higher earnings and better job opportunities. However, relying solely on human capital is risky because it is closely tied to your ability to work, and it has an expiry date unfortunately!

# Financial Capital: Your Door to Having a Rewarding Life

**Make Your Money Work for You.** Imagine you have a small garden and you plant seeds in the hope that the seeds will become a plant one day that can provide more seeds. This is exactly what a financial asset can do.

Financial capital refers to whatever you purchase in the hope it will generate a source of income and/or capital growth for you. There is no limit as to what can be a financial asset but I have outlined some of the well-known ones below.

**Transferring Human Capital to Financial Capital.**
As you grow in your career/business and accumulate savings, it's crucial to consciously transfer some of your human capital into financial capital. This process involves investing your left over disposable income into financial assets that can grow independently of your labour. By doing so, you create a safety net that can support you in times of need and provide for your retirement. It is important to have this done consistently and in a systematic fashion to ensure you have a rewarding and fulfilling life. You don't want to cheat your future self and at the same time, you don't want to enslave your current self.

# Understanding Asset Classes

Smart investing involves diversifying your portfolio across various asset classes to balance risk and return. Asset classes, as the name implies, are a class of assets you can invest in. These asset classes have different levels of risk and return and range from simple to complex. Understanding each one is your foundation to understand investing and how you can increase your financial capital. At different stages of life, you may prefer one asset class over the other, however, preference should not trump wisdom. As a community, lots of people favour one asset class, usually property, over other but this actually leads to suboptimal outcomes.

Here are the primary asset classes to consider:

# Defensive Assets

These assets usually don't grow significantly over time as they are more to defend against bad times when the general value of most assets fall in value. They are there for the provision of stability and income.

## 1. Cash and Cash Equivalents

- **Definition:** This is literally cash in the bank and can also be highly liquid, non risky assets that can be easily converted to cash or are actually cash. Usually if you are getting a growth or interest rate significantly higher than the Reserve Bank Cash Rate - this is not 'non risky'. Any rate more than 10 to 20% more than the cash rate has an element of undisclosed risk embedded in it.

- **Examples:** Savings accounts, money market funds.

- **Pros:** Very low risk, highly liquid (easily utilised for transactions).

- **Cons:** Low returns, vulnerable to inflation.

- **Example:** Your savings account at the Commonwealth Bank is a cash equivalent. It's safe, but you're not going to get rich from the interest it earns. You will barely even keep up with inflation with this asset. Cash is a psychological menace as you feel comfortable but are really shooting yourself in the foot. There is a limit of cash to be held and tax is paid on the interest you earn on this, another aspect many people don't consider.

## 2. Bonds and Other Fixed Interest

- **Definition:** Debt securities that pay periodic interest and return the principal at maturity. A simple way to think about this is you lending money to an institution and them promising to return this to you at a future date while  providing some periodic payments (coupons).

- **Examples:** Government bonds, corporate bonds.

- **Pros:** Steady income, lower risk compared to equities. This is low risk as in the unfortunate event of liquidation/bankruptcy of an institution, the bond holders are paid before the equity holders.

- **Cons:** Interest rate risk, lower potential returns. Bonds are actually one of the most complex asset classes as there are several aspects to think about. To mention a few - yield to maturity, duration, convertibility, callable or putable - these make it complex and usually very inefficient to invest directly in them to build your own portfolio.

- **Example:** Australian Government Bonds are considered very safe, providing regular interest payments, but their returns are modest compared to stocks. Bonds from a developing country won't be as safe because of government and legislative risk in those countries.

## 3. Annuities

Annuities are a sub-asset class that requires a section for itself. It helps in so many aspects and can be used by people at different stages in life.

- **Definition:** These are contracts with insurance companies that provide regular payments, typically for retirees, offering a steady income stream. They usually have a statutory fund (a fund that is regulated by the government to ensure they invest in just relatively low risk assets and have enough to withstand a mass exodus of clients).

- **Examples:** Fixed annuities, variable annuities, market linked annuities.

- **Pros:** Guaranteed income, potential tax benefits, Customisable payout options, longevity risk benefits (it helps you ensure you don't run out of money), estate planning benefits especially around age care.

- **Cons:** Limited liquidity, potentially lower returns compared to other investments.

- Examples:

  ◦ A fixed annuity from Generation Life might provide a steady income stream during retirement but usually comes with penalties for early withdrawal.

  ◦ An aged care annuity from Challenger Annuity can be purchased by an individual and they nominate specific beneficiaries to get the funds when they are to pass away. This usually bypasses the estate and Will so it usually cannot be contested.

  ◦ A lifetime annuity is purchased by an individual who has assets just above the cut-off for the age pension on the asset test to get some age pension and also get income for life from this life annuity.

## 4. Private Fixed Interest

- **Definition:** These are debt investments that are not publicly traded, often involving lending money to private companies or projects.

- **Examples:** Private debt, mezzanine debt, structured notes, venture debt, special situations.

- **Pros:** Higher potential returns than public bonds, Diversification benefits, Steady income.

- **Cons:** Higher risk of default, Limited liquidity, Complex investment structures, not available to the general public, high entry amounts.

- Example:

  ◦ Jane has 2 millions dollars to invest. She would like tailored exposure to a private fixed interest, so we put her in a La Trobe 4 year investment account with a minimum entry of $250k that can yield 8.4% pa at a variable rate.

  ◦ John wants to put funds in a mezzanine fund that can allow him to convert his private fixed interest rights (debt) to equities for this private company that is raising funds to get out of a settled legal case.

## 5. Defensive Alternatives

Alternatives are a large group of assets which are very heterogeneous, so there are many alternatives several professionals might not know about. However, having the basic understanding can help you spot the difference.

- **Definition:** Investments that aim to provide steady returns and capital preservation, often with lower correlation to traditional asset classes like stocks and bonds.

- **Examples:** Infrastructure debt, real estate debt, hedge funds focused on fixed income strategies.

- **Pros:** Diversification from traditional assets, potential for stable and predictable returns, lower volatility.

- **Cons:** High fees, limited transparency, complexity in understanding the investment strategies.

- **Example:** A client is investing in an infrastructure debt fund that finances toll roads and utility projects in Australia (IFM Investors Australian Infrastructure Debt Fund). This can provide stable returns with lower volatility, but it involves higher fees and complex investment structures.

# Growth Asset Classes

These assets, as the name implies, can grow over time, allowing you to significantly increase your wealth. It is important to understand the basics about each and the risks that come with them as well.

## 1. Property

- **Definition:** This is when you have ownership of a physical real estate asset. They are one of the most favoured assets across the world as it is easy to understand the basics. People will always need a home, office, or storage. Real estate investments include residential, commercial, and industrial properties. While real estate is the most known, it is not the most profitable, especially when no debt (gearing) is used. It is also very heterogeneous which makes it difficult to value accurately, and combined with the illiquidity, it can provide wrong valuations if not done professionally.

- **Pros:** Potential for capital appreciation, rental income, very easy to get loans on.

- **Cons**: Illiquid, requires significant capital.

- **Example:** Investing in a rental property in Sydney can provide steady income, but selling the property can take time.

## 2. Infrastructure

- **Definition:** These are large physical projects that are similar to real estate but not the same. They are investments in physical systems and structures needed for the operation of a society. There are several ways to invest in an infrastructural project; direct investment (best value due to illiquidity risk premium - in other words, you get an additional return for agreeing to lock your funds away), infrastructural funds (if invested in closed funds, this can be very advantageous), listed infrastructural companies (includes ETFs), REITS, public-private partnerships (great value as well).

- **Examples:** Roads, bridges, utilities (waste management, telecommunication networks), airports, ports.

- **Pros:** Stable, long-term returns, inflation hedge.

- **Cons:** High entry cost (usually for the best value investments), regulatory risks.

- **Example:** Investing in Transurban, which operates toll roads in Australia, provides steady returns but involves high initial investment and regulatory challenges.

## 3. Equities (International and Domestic)

- **Definition:** This is another well-known asset class. It is basically you owning a part of a company, which is called a share or equity. If a company has 1,000 shares and you own 100 of those, you own 10% of the company and you are ultimately the boss of the CEO. You can make decisions on who leads the company which is crucial for a successful company or investment generally. These shares can be in international or domestic listed companies (the general public can invest in them). I always explain the value of a company can easily grow more than that of a house or any assets above, but it can as much get to zero in value as well. Shares are a wonderful way to build wealth over time or even in a short period (which can be hard to understand when it seems like we only hear of the minute amount who make it).

- **Examples:** Domestic stocks, international stocks, emerging market stocks.

- **Pros:** High potential returns, dividends, easily accessible.

- **Cons:** Market volatility, economic risk, company specific risk, exchange rate risk.

- **Example:** Investing in BHP Group (BHP) offers high returns but comes with market risks and fluctuations. Investing in Tesla stocks can offer a high return with the risk as well.

## 4. Derivatives

- **Definition:** Just as the name implies, these are financial instruments deriving their value from underlying assets. Because of the derivation of the value, it requires thorough understanding of not just the derivative itself but also the underlying asset.

- **Examples:** Options, futures.

- **Pros:** Hedging risk, leverage - with derivatives you can leverage your investments without actually needing to borrow funds from anywhere to do this i.e. you don't need a lender to assess your ability to get a loan nor pay loan repayments.

- **Cons:** very complex, high risk.

- **Example:** Using stock options to hedge against potential losses can protect your portfolio but involves understanding complex strategies.

## 5. Private Equity

- **Definition:** This is one of the most affordable ways the average individual can build significant wealth over time. These are investments in private companies not listed on public exchanges. The benefit about this is usually they are people you know and trust and run a small business. These businesses can grow significantly over time and produce you wealth. You need to be invited to invest in these companies, hence the private nature.

- **Pros:** High potential returns, control over investments.

- **Cons:** High illiquidity, high risk.

- Example:
  - Investing in a startup through a venture capital firm like Blackbird Ventures can yield high returns, but there's a significant risk that the startup may fail.
  - Investing in a friend's small business. For example, a friend might be running a small tech startup and they have always been super diligent and visionary, and now need more capital to expand.
    - Pro tips for investing in small businesses:
      - They should be running for at least 2 years, have a vision, and importantly, a plan to achieve this vision.
      - They must be cash flow positive, it is not ideal to put money in a small business that cannot generate cash flow for itself.
      - They should provide a business valuation to you from an independent source. Value now, not potential value. This doesn't mean you need to pay just the value now but it is a good anchor to have.
      - Have a documented exit plan that suits both parties.
      - Understand the industry or speak to an expert around this to get a good understanding.
      - Take the risk. The general stats show that 85% of high-net-worth individuals amassed their wealth by starting or owning stakes in a business (the point is this usually starts small).

# 6. Commodities

- **Definition:** These are investments that are directly or indirectly related to raw materials which are usually called hard commodities, or primary agricultural products like wheat, corn, or cattle which are called soft commodities.

- **Examples:** Gold, oil, agricultural products.

- **Pros:** Inflation hedge, diversification.

- **Cons:** Volatility, no income generation.

- Example:

  ○ Buying gold through the Perth Mint can protect against inflation, but it doesn't generate income like dividends or interest.

  ○ Buying live cattle in a farm.

  ○ You can also purchase commodity stocks on the stock exchange.

# 7. Bonus Asset Class - Digital Assets

- **Definition:** These assets encompass a wide range of items that exist in a digital form and are typically managed through a blockchain technology. Blockchain has made these assets really valuable and I argue the value is more in the blockchain than in these assets themselves. However, in a classic demand vs supply situation, demand has led these assets to become very valuable. In the finance world, these are not regulated assets as of yet but I am confident they will be soon and will fit somewhere in this space of financial assets. For now, it is worth exploring these for clearer understanding.

- **Blockchain:** Blockchain technology is a secure and transparent way to record transactions, ensuring data integrity and trust. It helps create digital assets like tokens using smart contracts on platforms such as Ethereum. These smart contracts define and launch tokens, which can be sold to investors through Initial Coin Offerings (ICOs), with all transactions recorded on the blockchain.

  Blockchain ensures security through decentralisation, where multiple computers (nodes) hold copies of the blockchain, making it nearly impossible for a single point of failure. This decentralisation makes the data tamper-proof and publicly visible, reducing the risk of fraud.

Blockchain is widely used in various areas:

- **Cryptocurrencies:** Bitcoin uses blockchain to record transactions, preventing double spending and ensuring the integrity of the currency.

- **Tokens:** Ethereum's smart contracts create various tokens used in finance, gaming, and other applications.

- **NFTs:** Platforms like OpenSea use blockchain to ensure the uniqueness and ownership of digital items such as art and collectibles.

- **Supply Chain:** Blockchain tracks the origins and movements of goods, ensuring authenticity and reducing fraud.

Blockchain technology provides a secure, transparent, and decentralised way to create and manage digital assets, protecting them from fraud and unauthorised access.

- **Pros:** High potential returns, diversification.

- **Cons:** Extreme volatility, regulatory uncertainty.

## Digital Assets Categories Table

| Category | Subcategory | Examples | Description |
|---|---|---|---|
| Cyptocurrencies | Payment Coins | Bitcoin (BTC), Litecoin (LTC) | Digital currencies primarily used as a medium of exchange and store of value. |
| | Platform Coins | Ethereum (ETH), Cardano (ADA) | Cryptocurrencies that provide infrastructure for other decentralised apps. |
| | Privacy Coins | Monero (XMR), ZCash (ZEC) | Cryptocurrencies focusing on enhanced transaction privacy and anonymity. |
| Tokens | Utility Tokens | Filecoin (FIL), Basic Attention Token (BAT) | Provide access to a product or service within a blockchain ecosystem. |
| | Security Tokens | tZERO, Securitise | Represent ownership in an asset, like shares in a company or real estate. |
| | Stablecoins | Tether (USDT), USD Coin (USDC) | Pegged to a stable asset like the US dollar to reduce volatility. |
| | Non-Fungible Tokens (NFTs) | CryptoPunks, Bored Ape Yacht Club, NBA Top Shot | Unique tokens representing ownership of specific items or digital content. |
| Other Digital Assets | Digital Real Estate | Decentraland (LAND), The Sandbox (SAND) | Ownership and trading of virtual land and properties in metaverses. |
| | Digital Identity Tokens | Civic (CVC), SelfKey (KEY) | Used to verify identities online securely. |
| | Digital Collectibles | Axie Infinity, Gods Unchained | Unique tokens representing ownership of specific items or digital content. |

# Ways to invest and make your money work

## Investing in Direct Shares

I feel this is an inefficient way for someone to invest if it is not your day time job. However, I will feed your curiosity. Investing in direct shares requires thorough analysis and due diligence. Here are five critical aspects to watch out for before buying any company's stock:

## 1. Debt of the Company (Debt to Equity)

- A high debt-to-equity ratio can indicate financial instability. Look for companies with manageable debt levels. This varies from industry to industry but a good gauge is it should be less than that of the industry. This shows they are more prudent in that regard. There are a few companies that will have a high amount of debt compared to the industry. While this is not a deal breaker, it requires a thorough understanding of why they have this higher amount. I will not encourage you to go deeper into the maturity date of these liabilities but that is something that you can drill down on if needed. As of 2024, companies that have a shorter time to pay back might face higher borrowing costs/renegotiations with their lenders as we have had a large interest rate increase over the last year.

- **Example:** A company like Woolworths Group (WOW) has a manageable debt level relative to its equity, indicating financial stability.

| Industry | Country | Debt to Equity Ratio |
|---|---|---|
| Mining | Australia | 0.45 |
| Healthcare | Australia | 0.75 |
| Financials | Australia | 1.20 |
| Consumer Discretionary | Australia | 0.65 |
| Industrials | Australia | 0.80 |
| Mining | USA | 0.50 |
| Healthcare | USA | 0.60 |
| Financials | USA | 1.50 |
| Consumer Discretionary | USA | 0.70 |
| Industrials | USA | 0.90 |

## 2. Dividends Received, Payout Ratios, and Yield

- Dividends is one of my must haves. If a company is not paying dividends, I don't invest in them directly. I learnt this value investing concept from The Intelligent Investor. There is also a psychological benefit as you get something back from your investment every 6 months which can then be used for more opportunities with the same company or others. In a high mortgage rate environment with low opportunities to buy more stocks, the funds can be kept in your offset account. Evidence shows that companies paying dividends at a reasonable rate (as I will explain below) stay in business longer and are more efficient.

  There is also the other side of the coin, where they generally don't grow as much as growth companies. However, if you buy at a discount, you automatically get double the benefit of a locked-in gain (not a potential gain that growth companies have embedded in the price) and the return you get on the dividends is also locked in. For example, in the last crisis during COVID, those who were informed enough and had the resources to buy when values were at a discount benefited a lot. Take buying Nick Scali at $5 a share in 2020 with a dividend return of $0.75 as of now. You get a return of 15% on your investment excluding dividend imputation. Buying a value company's stock when it is low allows you to benefit from the share's growth, currently $14.04 (a 180% gain). While these opportunities don't come in this magnitude every time, they still present themselves often enough.

- **Payout ratios** are important as well, which is the amount paid out from the company's profits. A company cannot maintain, over a long period of time, paying out more than they earn. This is akin to spending more than you earn, it is not sustainable. Anywhere between 40 to 70% is a decent payout ratio. This is not a hard-and-fast rule, so if a company has sold part of its assets or subsidiaries, they can be in a position to pay out a higher percentage for a short period of time.

- **Dividend yield** is a financial ratio that indicates how much a company pays out in dividends each year relative to its share price. It is expressed as a percentage and is used by investors to gauge the return on investment from dividends alone. A high dividend yield can be seen in certain industries over others and this may just be a nature of the business. Generally companies with high dividend yields won't have high growth opportunities.

- ◦ **Example:** See table below for some examples

| Industry | Country | Dividend Payout Ratio (%) | Dividend Yield (%) | High Yield Company | High Yield (%) |
|---|---|---|---|---|---|
| Mining | Australia | 55 | 3.5 | BHP Group | 5.5 |
| Healthcare | Australia | 60 | 4.0 | CSL Limited | 1.5 |
| Financials | Australia | 70 | 5.0 | Commonwealth Bank | 4.8 |
| Consumer Discretionary | Australia | 50 | 3.0 | Wesfarmers | 3.2 |
| Industrials | Australia | 65 | 4.5 | Transurban | 4.0 |
| Mining | USA | 50 | 3.0 | Newmont Corporation | 3.5 |
| Healthcare | USA | 55 | 3.5 | Johnson & Johnson | 2.6 |
| Financials | USA | 60 | 4.5 | JPMorgan Chase | 3.0 |
| Consumer Discretionary | USA | 50 | 3.0 | Amazon | 0.0 |
| Industrials | USA | 60 | 4.0 | Caterpillar | 2.5 |

## 3. Revenue Growth and Expense Trajectory

- ◦ The revenue of the company is the total proceeds from the sale of their company's services or products. In an ideal world, we want the revenue of the company to be growing and the total expenses of the business going down. This will translate into the profits, which is what the shareholders get, to increase over time. When you find a company that can do this, it will be a very profitable investment. In reality, there are very few companies that do this consistently over the years. The bare minimum is a company that has grown its revenue over the last 5 years consistently or reduced total expenses in that same period.

  You need to have wiggle room, as things happen to companies just like anything in life. For example, most companies had reductions in revenue during COVID, and only a few were able to grow their sales. So, if you are looking at a company and you know there was a known event that affected the industry, you should not mark this aspect down just due to that year.

- ◦ On the contrary, companies that bounced straight back after such events like COVID or other financial crises should be viewed as good companies. Steady revenue growth coupled with controlled expenses suggests a healthy, growing company.

- ○ **Example:** CSL Limited (CSL) has shown significant revenue growth over the years while managing expenses effectively, contributing to its overall growth.

| Company | Industry | Country | Revenue Growth | Expense Reduction |
|---------|----------|---------|----------------|-------------------|
| NVIDIA Corporation (NVDA) | Technology | USA | High | Yes |
| Johnson & Johnson (JNJ) | Healthcare | USA | Steady | Yes |
| Microsoft Corporation (MSFT) | Technology | USA | Strong | Yes |
| Apple Inc. (AAPL) | Technology | USA | Steady | Yes |
| Procter & Gamble (PG) | Consumer Goods | USA | Steady | Yes |
| Commonwealth Bank (CBA) | Financials | Australia | Steady | Yes |
| BHP Group (BHP) | Mining | Australia | Strong | Yes |
| CSL Limited (CSL) | Healthcare | Australia | Steady | Yes |
| Wesfarmers (WES) | Consumer Goods | Australia | Moderate | Yes |
| Woolworths Group (WOW) | Retail | Australia | Steady | Yes |

# 4. Cash Flow

- ○ Cash flow is another important criterion to look at. Companies can become bankrupt even if they are in a profitable position. This is why you need to understand their cash flow position. There are 3 aspects to cash flow: the operation, investing, and financing cash flow. The net amount of these can be added together to see how the bank account is tracking. It is more complex than this but in the interest of keeping it simple, as long as this amount is consistently positive, it is okay to have this aspect ticked. If cash flow is consistently negative, you want to explore further to see why this is the case. It might be one of the following:

  i. They are investing in new equipment.

  ii. They have too much cash and are looking to invest in paying down debt or growing the business by investing in another company.

  iii. They are buying stocks back or paying out dividends higher than usual.

If none of the above, it deserves you looking deeper into this. Generally if this is the case and it is negative more on the investing and financing side, it is of less concern than if it was from the operating side. Operating cash flow is from the core business and should generally be the positive cash flow to help support the rest.

Other ratios are snapshots but are worth looking at:

- **Quick Ratio:** Measures a company's ability to meet its short-term obligations using its most liquid assets, excluding inventory. Higher than industry average indicates better liquidity.

- **Current Ratio:** Measures a company's ability to meet its short-term obligations using all current assets. Higher than industry average indicates overall better liquidity.

Example:

- **Apple Inc. (USA):**
  - **Quick Ratio:** 1.6 (Above industry average of 1.5)
  - **Current Ratio:** 1.9 (Above industry average of 1.8)
  - **Interpretation:** Apple has better immediate and overall liquidity compared to the average technology company.

- **Commonwealth Bank of Australia (Australia):**
  - **Quick Ratio:** 0.8 (Above industry average of 0.7)
  - **Current Ratio:** 1.2 (Above industry average of 1.1)
  - **Interpretation:** Commonwealth Bank has better liquidity compared to the average financial services company in Australia.

These examples illustrate how companies compare to their industry peers in terms of liquidity, providing insight into their financial health.

We don't want the company to run out of money in the bank, so cash should be sufficient to cover costs.

| Company | Country | Industry | Quick Ratio | Current Ratio | Industry Average Quick Ratio | Industry Average Quick Ratio |
|---|---|---|---|---|---|---|
| Commonwealth Banf of Australia | Australia | Financial Services | 0.8 | 1.2 | 0.7 | 1.1 |
| BHP Group | Australia | Mining | 1.2 | 1.5 | 1.1 | 1.4 |
| CSL Limited | Australia | Healthcare | 1.5 | 2.0 | 1.4 | 1.9 |
| Wesfarmers | Australia | Consumer Goods | 0.7 | 1.0 | 0.6 | 0.9 |
| Woolworths Group | Australia | Retail | 0.9 | 1.3 | 0.8 | 1.2 |
| Apple Inc. | USA | Technology | 1.6 | 1.9 | 1.5 | 1.8 |
| Microsoft Corporation | USA | Technology | 2.5 | 2.7 | 2.3 | 2.6 |
| Johnson & Johnson | USA | Healthcare | 1.2 | 1.5 | 1.1 | 1.4 |
| Amazon.com | USA | Consumer Goods | 0.9 | 1.1 | 0.8 | 1.0 |
| Protector & Gamble | USA | Consumer Goods | 1.0 | 1.2 | 0.9 | 1.1 |

## 5. Leadership of the Company

- ◦ **Explanation:** Strong, ethical leadership is crucial for long-term success. Research the track record and reputation of the company's executives. Companies that have changed leadership too often are not ideal, not just because it indicates there might be a bad culture, but also, it doesn't give the leader time to make impactful changes. You need time to change things for the long-term benefit of the company, community, and shareholders.

  Look at the history and experience of the leaders and board members. Iron sharpens iron and bad leadership usually follows a bad leader.

- ◦ **Example:** Macquarie Group (MQG) under the leadership of Shemara Wikramanayake has shown remarkable growth, though it's essential to consider the associated risks with such leadership.

  In all the aspects above, analysing a 5-year history gives you a clear enough picture to make a good decision. Why 5 years? It is hard for a company to manipulate data for 5 years and this gives time to really ensure it is sustainable change/figures they have put in place.

**Time-Consuming Nature of Individual Stock Analysis -** Analysing individual stocks is labour-intensive and requires continuous monitoring. Investigating about eight companies thoroughly can be a part-time job by itself, which might not be feasible for everyone. Stock picking sounds great and you hear of the great stories of winners, but you are more likely to benefit from increasing your human capital for your chosen career. Use comparative advantage to make better decisions.

## Comparative Advantage

**Specialised Field Advantage -** If you have a specialised field or career, focus on building your human capital and consider delegating investment management to professionals. This allows you to leverage your expertise for maximum earnings while benefiting from expert financial management.

Imagine Dr. Smith, an exceptional surgeon who could also excel in engineering, finance, or law. However, focusing on surgery, where Dr. Smith earns $2,000 per hour, is more efficient than spending time in other fields where the earnings are lower. By concentrating on surgery,

Dr. Smith maximises income and productivity. Instead of diversifying into other professions, Dr. Smith hires engineers, financial advisors, and lawyers. This specialisation leverages Dr. Smith's strengths and ensures optimal use of time and resources, embodying the principle of comparative advantage. Even if Dr. Smith has time to invest, I argue she should spend time on her health and relationships. No one can work out in the gym or spend quality time with family for you, so comparative advantage is limited in those areas of life.

# Investing in Curated Portfolios

Investing in curated portfolios, portfolios that have the asset allocations set and the individual assets chosen for you is a more efficient way to create wealth and frees your time up for activities that are fulfilling for you. There are different ways to invest in these portfolios and each has their pros and cons.

## ETFs vs. Managed Funds

- **ETFs (Exchange-Traded Funds):**
  - A type of fund that owns a basket of assets and is traded on stock exchanges. ETFs can be bought and sold on a brokerage account like a normal stock but this is a basket, so it is diversified and can be a good way to invest in all the asset classes mentioned above. A huge benefit of ETFs is the ability to trade straight away on platform/brokerage. These are live trades, so quicker trades for quick decisions can be made.
  - **Pros:** Low fees, liquidity, transparency, quicker trades, low investment amount needed.
  - **Cons:** Market risk, tracking errors, access to less actively managed funds, brokerage costs, hard to have funds that have 100% diversified growth allocation.
  - **Example:** The SPDR S&P/ASX 200 ETF (STW) tracks the ASX 200 index and offers low-cost exposure to the Australian stock market.

- **Managed Funds:**
  - Professionally managed investment funds that pool money from multiple investors. Trades are not executed straight away, so opportunities for making a quick buy when there is an intraday opportunity is not possible.

- **Pros:** Professional management, diversification, access to more curated investments portfolios.

- **Cons:** Slower trades, cannot be done live, not as liquid as ETFs, higher initial investment amount needed.

- **Example:** Platinum International Fund (PIATX) is a managed fund that aims to outperform the market by selecting high-quality growth stocks.

## Diversification and Time Management

Investing in funds provides instant diversification and is a time-efficient way to manage your portfolio. You gain exposure to a broad range of assets without the need to research and manage each one individually.

# Active vs. Passive Management

- **Passive/Index Funds:**
  - **Definition:** Funds that track a market index.
  - **Pros:** Low fees, consistent performance linked to the market.
  - **Cons:** Limited flexibility.
  - **Example:** Vanguard Australian Shares Index Fund (VAS) offers broad market exposure with low fees.

- **Active Management:**
  - **Definition:** Funds managed by professionals who actively select investments.
  - **Pros:** Potential for higher returns, especially in non-western markets, small companies, specialised industries and alternatives.
  - **Cons:** Higher fees, performance risk.
  - **Example:** Magellan Global Fund focuses on active management in global markets, aiming to outperform passive indexes.

# Market Capitalisation and Stock Types

## Market Capitalisation

- **Large Caps:** Established companies with a market cap usually over $10 billion.
  - **Pros:** Stability, dividends.
  - **Cons:** Slower growth.
  - **Example:** Commonwealth Bank of Australia (CBA) is a large-cap company known for its stability and regular dividend payouts.
- **Mid Caps:** Companies with a market cap usually between $2 billion and $10 billion.
  - **Pros:** Growth potential, stability.
  - **Cons:** Moderately higher risk than large caps.
  - **Example:** REA Group (REA), the company behind realestate.com.au, is a mid-cap company that balances growth potential with relative stability.

- **Small Caps:** Companies with a market cap under $2 billion.
  - ◦ **Pros:** High growth potential.
  - ◦ **Cons:** Higher risk than Mid Caps.
  - ◦ **Example:** Afterpay (APT), before its acquisition, was a small-cap company that offered high growth potential but came with greater volatility.

## Stock Types

- **Value Stocks:** Undervalued companies with strong fundamentals.
  - ◦ **Pros:** Potential for appreciation.
  - ◦ **Cons:** May remain undervalued for a long time.
  - ◦ **Example:** Wesfarmers (WES) is often considered a value stock due to its strong fundamentals and steady performance.
- **Growth Stocks:** Companies expected to grow at an above-average rate.
  - ◦ **Pros:** High potential returns.
  - ◦ **Cons:** High volatility.
  - ◦ **Example:** Xero Limited (XRO) is a growth stock with substantial revenue growth, but it also experiences high volatility.

## Conclusion

Investing wisely requires a balanced approach, combining human capital investment with strategic financial investments. By understanding different asset classes, analysing direct shares, and utilising funds for diversification, you can build a robust portfolio tailored to your financial goals. Always consider seeking professional advice to complement your expertise and optimise your investment strategy. Remember, the ultimate goal is to transform your hard-earned human capital into stable and growing financial capital that secures your future.

By leveraging your unique skills and knowledge while investing strategically, you can achieve financial stability and growth, ensuring a secure and prosperous future.

> *Meet Mr. Market, your attention-seeking drama queen. He is very good at throwing tantrums with every market report, tweet, rumour, or even just a cloudy day. The less diversified you are, the more Mr. Market acts out, feeling entitled to every bit of your attention. Sometimes good and funny, money making tantrums, sometimes at the huge opposite end.*

> *But here's the trick: diversify your investments. Spread your bets across different sectors, and Mr. Market starts to behave better. He still craves attention, but with a diversified portfolio, his tantrums are less impactful. And if you can ignore his antics long enough, usually a few years, he tends to reward your patience. He is just like that and he knows it!*

> *In short, handle Mr. Market like the diva he is. Diversify to keep his tantrums in check, and watch as your investments grow despite his attention-seeking ways.*

That is how I sum up the markets and investments for most people, as we have all seen or dealt with a drama queen before.

# CHAPTER 5

# PERSONAL PROTECTION - SECURING YOUR FUTURE, LOVED ONES' FUTURE AND PEACE OF MIND

# STRATEGY 5 –
# PROTECT YOUR HUMAN CAPITAL. ENSURE YOU HAVE PROTECTION FOR UNFORESEEN EVENTS THAT ARE LIFE CHANGING!

## Introduction: Shielding Your Tomorrow Today

Imagine waking up one morning to find that your world has turned upside down. The unforeseen has happened, and without the right protection, your financial stability and the well-being of your loved ones are at risk. Welcome to the world of personal protection – where safeguarding your assets, your income, and your family's future isn't just a plan, but a necessity. I have had fit and fully sane people walk into my office one minute and the next, their situations have totally changed. Some with the understanding to be protected and get cover, others unfortunate enough to not have cover who wish they had covered themselves for millions of dollars earlier.

Death, serious sickness, and injury can happen to anyone at any time. The only reason you should not get cover is because you are self insured. Don't joke around with this.

# Why Personal Protection is Crucial

Life is unpredictable, and while we cannot foresee every challenge, we can prepare for the crucial ones. Protecting your assets ensures that your hard-earned wealth is safe, and your loved ones are provided for in case of an unfortunate event. Here are some key reasons why personal protection is a must:

1.  **Providing for Loved Ones:** Ensuring your family is financially secure even when you're not around.

2.  **Preventing Financial Burden:** Avoiding the situation where your loved ones have to shoulder your financial responsibilities. One of the most painful cases is when you become disabled or ill and cannot provide for them, or even just yourself if you have no loved ones dependent on you.

3.  **Maintaining Living Standards:** Making sure that you and your family's lifestyle remains unchanged if your earning capacity is compromised.

4.  **Transferring Human Capital:** Ensuring you can still get some of the human capital you would have gotten if you were not injured or ill.

# Life Insurance

Life insurance is a cornerstone of personal protection. It provides a financial safety net for your loved ones in the event of your untimely death. The need for life insurance typically follows a bell curve – it is highest when you are young and have dependents, and it decreases as you age and your financial obligations lessen.

### Key Questions to Determine Life Insurance Needs:

How many dependents do you have?

What are your current debts and liabilities and would someone need to shoulder these for you? Would there be a net amount left or just an unwanted burden?

What are your family's living expenses and future financial goals?

- ◦ Do your dependents have future financial needs, such as for education, buying a home, or marriages?

How much do you want to leave behind for your loved ones?

- ◦ You might not want to leave anything behind for loved ones but generally it is cheaper to have life insurance linked to TPD so you can leave the funds to charity.

For some high-net-worth individuals, this is actually a way to help even out inheritance for beneficiaries. See appendix - 5.1.

# Total and Permanent Disability (TPD) Insurance

TPD insurance covers you if you are permanently unable to work due to injury or illness. Like life insurance, the need for TPD insurance follows a bell curve. It peaks when you are young and have high financial commitments and decreases as you approach retirement. The rule is if two independent medical professionals say you are unlikely to return to work in the foreseeable future, you can get a claim paid out.

The most prevalent case we see these days is mental health issue claims. Comprehensive insurers are critical of people with any previous episodes but it is still possible to not get an exclusion. An exclusion is when they cover you but will not pay out cover for a specific illness or injury. I always prefer a loading in such cases but it is not up to me to decide. A loading is when they just charge you a higher premium because of a specific issue.

### Key Questions to Determine TPD Insurance Needs:

What is your current income and for how long would you need it to be replaced?

Do you have any existing health conditions?

What are your long-term financial obligations and goals?

What level of financial support would your family need if you were unable to work?

Who would take care of you?

Do you need replacements or modifications done to the place you currently live in? Especially if you own the place.

What are out of pocket medical costs?

- Things not covered by Medicare, NDIS nor private health insurance are:
    - Specialised equipment for use (wheelchairs and prosthetics).
    - Therapy for mental health.
    - Specialised consults.

# Trauma Protection

Trauma insurance provides a lump sum payment if you are diagnosed with a critical illness like cancer, stroke, or heart disease. The need for trauma insurance also follows a bell curve, reducing as you age and your financial responsibilities decrease. A myth about trauma cover is that it is only needed as you get older but in fact it is needed as soon as you start working.

Locking in a lower rate at a younger age can be very beneficial as the price gets more expensive as you get older. Examples of traumatic events usually claimed by people under 35 are melanoma and severe burns.

**Key Questions to Determine Trauma Insurance Needs:**

Who will take care of you during this time?

What are your existing health conditions and family medical history?

How much might medical treatment and recovery cost?

What are your ongoing living expenses or debt repayments?

How much financial support would your family need during your recovery?

## Income Protection

This is by far the most important and really caters to your human capital preservation. Your income helps you get any other insurance, pays your bills and helps you live the life you want. Have it covered.

Income protection insurance ensures that you continue to receive a portion of your income if you are unable to work due to illness or injury. Unlike the previous insurances, the need for income protection lasts until you fully retire, as it replaces your income and helps maintain your lifestyle.

### Key Questions to Determine Income Protection Needs:

What is your current income and monthly expenses?

How long could you sustain your lifestyle without your current income?

- ◦ There is a balance, as you don't want to spend all your savings if you couldn't work for 1 to 2 years, you should not unless absolutely needed. You might even consider reducing the amount you are covered for vs increasing the time period you get paid (waiting period).

The longer you wait the cheaper the policies but the larger the risk. The lower you are covered for, the lower premiums you pay but also the larger the risk. Balancing this appropriately is an art.

What other sources of income or savings do you have?

When do you plan to retire?

A really smart friend of mine suffered serious mental issues from the age of 25. He was lucky to have some protection in place to help him sustain his living standard. He was smashing university and started a great job and really was set to go places until this happened. It can happen to anyone, be protected.

# Buy/Sell Insurance

Your business partner's spouse is the life of the party and really cares for people around them. However, they don't have the skills of your business partner. Imagine them inheriting the share of the business and you have to then have a new business partner who cannot provide any value to the business. Not only have you lost your business partner, you are in a position of needing financial assistance to buy off the share of your late/disabled business partner from their spouse. If they agree to sell this to you.

Buy/sell insurance is essential for business owners. It ensures that if a partner dies or becomes permanently disabled, the remaining partners can buy their share of the business without financial strain.

**Key Questions to Determine Buy/Sell Insurance Needs:**

What is the current value of your business?

What are the terms of your buy/sell agreement?

How many partners are involved and what are their stakes?

What financial impact would the loss of a partner have on the business?

What is the ownership of the protection in place?

If you are in business with a business partner, sort out your voluntary and involuntary business succession plan.

## Keyman/Keywoman Protection

The loss of key personnel in a business can be very detrimental. Sometimes for small business owners, this person is you. Other times it is another team member. Keyman/woman insurance protects a business against the loss of a key employee. The insurance provides a payout to help the business recover and find a replacement, ensuring continuity and stability.

**Key Questions to Determine Keyman Insurance Needs:**

Who are the key employees critical to your business operations?

What is the financial contribution of these key employees to the business?

What would be the cost of finding and training a replacement?

How long would it take for the business to recover from the loss of a key employee?

## Steps to Getting the Right Cover

1. **Insurance Needs Analysis:** Evaluate your financial situation, dependents, debts, and future needs to determine the right amount and type of insurance. The questions above can help you get to the right amount. It is really hard to do this yourself so get help or tools that prompt you.

   Good tools to use are:

   **Australian:**

   a. https://www.mlc.com.au/personal/insurance/insurance-estimator

   b. https://insurance.aia.com.au/AIAInsuranceNeedsWebService/ui/

   **International:**

   A. https://www.securian.com/insights-tools/life-insurance-needs-calculator.html

   B. https://www.massmutual.com/financial-wellness/calculators

   These tools don't even touch the surface of getting it done properly though.

2. **Choosing the Right Structure:**

   a. When planning your financial safety net, choosing between funding insurance premiums from your superannuation or from your own pocket is pivotal. Here's a structured guide to help you make an informed decision for both scenarios—inside and outside superannuation.

# Inside Superannuation

### Advantages of Paying Premiums from Superannuation:

- **Cash Flow Relief:** If your budget is tight, using superannuation to pay for premiums can alleviate immediate financial pressure, allowing you to maintain necessary coverage without impacting your daily finances.

- **Compound Benefits:** Should you need to claim, especially on policies like income protection, some plans allow for contributions to your superannuation during the claim period. This can significantly bolster your retirement funds even if you are not working.

### Cost vs. Benefit Analysis:

- **Scenario Modelling:** For a 35-year-old earning an average income of $105,000 plus superannuation contributions, investing in protection can lead to an estimated $1.5 million in super by age 65, with around $200,000 spent on premiums. Without insurance, the same individual might only accumulate $400,000 due to the financial impact of being unable to work.

- **Protection Impact:** With a structured income protection claim, it's projected you could still achieve approximately $1.05 million in super, showing a strategic advantage in having the policy.

# Outside Superannuation

### Benefits of External Insurance Payments:

- **Tax Advantages:** Holding your income protection outside of super can yield tax deductions, providing annual tax savings. For business owners, you can have some covers tax deductible if it is set up for business revenue protection purposes.

- **Financial Flexibility:** If cash flow is not an issue, paying for insurance outside of super allows you to keep your retirement savings intact and growing without the deduction of premium costs.

**Strategic Considerations for Life Stages:**

- **Younger Individuals:** It's generally more effective to have premiums taken from your retirement contributions without the burden of insurance premiums reducing your cash flow.

- **Approaching Retirement:** As retirement nears, maximising super contributions becomes a priority. At this stage, transitioning to having life and TPD insurance outside of super might make more sense to enhance your retirement readiness.

Understanding the implications of where and how you pay your insurance premiums—whether from superannuation or out-of-pocket—can significantly affect your financial health and retirement planning. It's crucial to consider these options with a comprehensive understanding of both immediate financial impacts and long-term benefits. Engaging with a financial advisor to tailor this decision to your personal circumstances and financial goals is highly recommended.

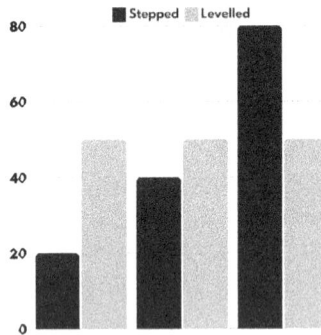

b. Stepped vs level premium structure. Usually only offered with comprehensive providers.

   i. **Stepped Premiums**

   **Definition:** Stepped premiums start lower and increase each year as you age.

   **How it Works:**

   - **Initial Cost:** The initial cost of stepped premiums is lower compared to level premiums.

   - **Annual Increases:** Premiums increase each year, reflecting the higher risk associated with ageing.

**Pros:**

- **Affordability:** Lower initial cost makes it more affordable for young policyholders.
- **Flexibility:** Good for short-term coverage needs or for those expecting to change their financial situation in the near future.

**Cons:**

- **Long-Term Cost:** Can become significantly more expensive over time, especially as the policyholder ages.
- **Budget Uncertainty:** Annual increases make it harder to predict long-term costs.

**Ideal For:** Younger individuals or those with shorter-term insurance needs who want to minimise initial costs.

ii. **Level Premiums**

**Definition:** Level premiums remain fairly constant throughout the life of the policy. There might be increases but a lot less than the stepped covers.

**How it Works:**

- **Consistent Payments:** Premiums are calculated to spread the cost evenly over the term of the policy.
- **Stable Budgeting:** Payments do not increase with age, providing predictability.

**Pros:**

- **Long-Term Savings:** More cost-effective over the long term as premiums do not increase directly with age.
- **Budget Stability:** Easier to plan financially with fixed premiums.

**Cons:**

- **Higher Initial Cost:** More expensive initially compared to stepped premiums.
- **Commitment:** Requires a longer-term commitment to maximise cost benefits.

**Ideal For:** Individuals seeking long-term coverage with predictable payments and those planning for the future stability of their insurance costs.

**Example Comparison**

**Scenario:** A 30-year-old considering a life insurance policy. For illustration only as in reality, it depends on amount covered, occupation and a lot more.

- **Stepped Premiums:**
  - **Age 30:** $20/month
  - **Age 40:** $40/month
  - **Age 50:** $80/month
  - **Total over 20 years:** Higher overall due to increasing costs.
- **Level Premiums:**
  - **Age 30-50:** $50/month
  - **Total over 20 years:** Lower overall if the individual maintains the policy for the full term.

## Choosing the Right Option Structure

**Considerations:**

- **Age and Health:** Younger, ambitious, healthier individuals might benefit from lower initial costs of stepped premiums but should be aware of future increases.
- **Financial Stability:** Those with stable long-term income may prefer the predictability of level premiums.
- **Coverage Duration:** Short-term needs might be better served with stepped premiums, while long-term needs align with level premiums.

Both stepped and level premiums offer unique advantages depending on your financial situation and insurance needs. Stepped premiums provide lower initial costs but increase over time, making them suitable for short-term needs or younger individuals. Level premiums offer stability and long-term savings, ideal for those planning for future financial predictability.

3. **Choosing the Right Insurer:** Select policies that provide adequate coverage for your specific needs. Here's a concise guide to help you make an informed decision:

   a. **Financial Stability and Reputation**

   **Importance:** Ensures the insurer is reliable and can honour claims.

   - **Check Ratings:** Look at ratings from agencies like Canstar, Insurance Watch Australia and Finder. Overseas you can check out Nerdwallet and Policy Genius.

   - **Review Reputation:** Research customer reviews, satisfaction ratings, and any history of complaints.

   b. **Coverage Options**

   **Importance:** Ensures the policy meets your specific needs.

   - **Range of Products:** Verify the insurer offers life, TPD, trauma, and income protection insurance.

   - **Customisation:** Look for policies that can be tailored to your unique needs.

   - **Riders and Add-Ons:** Check availability of additional coverage options like critical illness riders, claims indexation for income protection or waiver of premium.

   c. **Claim Settlement Ratio**

   **Importance:** Indicates the insurer's reliability in paying out claims.

   - **Claim Process:** Evaluate how straightforward and transparent the claim process is.

   - **Speed of Settlement:** Check average claim processing times.

   d. **Premium Costs**

   **Importance:** Ensures affordability and value for coverage offered.

   - **Compare Premiums:** Across multiple providers for similar coverage.

   - **Stepped vs. Level Premiums:** Understand the difference for long-term financial planning.

e. **Policy Features and Benefits**

**Importance:** Ensures comprehensive protection.

- **Coverage Limits:** Verify the sum insured is sufficient for your needs.
- **Exclusions and Limitations:** Be aware of any exclusions or limitations.

f. **Customer Service**

**Importance:** Ensures accessible help and support.

- **Accessibility:** Check availability of customer service through phone, email, and online chat.
- **Support Services:** Look for additional services like financial planning advice or health and wellness programs.

g. **Flexibility and Portability**

**Importance:** Allows policy adjustments as circumstances change.

- **Policy Adjustments:** Ability to adjust coverage levels or add riders as needed.
- **Portability:** Ensure the policy can be maintained if you change jobs or move.

By evaluating these criteria, you can make an informed decision and choose an insurance provider that best meets your needs for life, TPD, trauma, and income protection insurance.

Here are some providers offering comprehensive insurance covers:

- **Australia:**
  - Metlife
  - AIA Australia
  - Clearview
  - PPS Mutual
  - Zurich Australia
  - NEOS

- **USA:**
  - Prudential Financial
  - MetLife
  - Northwestern Mutual
  - New York Life
  - MassMutual

# Super Fund Covers

Superannuation funds often provide default cover for life, TPD, and income protection insurance. While these covers can be useful as a fallback, they are typically not underwritten, which means they usually offer less comprehensive protection and can be harder to claim on. Additionally, the coverage amount is often insufficient to meet all your needs.

**Why Super Fund Covers are Useful:**

- **Convenience:** People usually have this in place and never think about cover but are lucky to get a claim paid out if something was to happen.

- **Strategic Use:** If you are unable to get comprehensive cover, the default ones you have in your superannuation can be a plan B.

- **Adjusting Over Time:** Most of the ones in your super are automatically reduced over time and helps ensure you are not over insured. Over insurance is rarely the case with the default covers.

## Comprehensive Covers vs. Super Fund Covers

While the covers provided by your super fund and those outside are often from the same insurance companies, the terms and conditions can differ significantly. Comprehensive covers typically offer better terms, higher sums insured, and easier claims processes, making them more reliable despite the higher cost.

# Why Get Underwritten Cover?

## What is Underwriting?

Underwriting is the process insurers use to assess the risk of insuring you. They evaluate your health, lifestyle, and other factors to determine your premiums and coverage terms.

## Importance of Underwriting

Underwriting ensures that the insurance policy accurately reflects your risk profile. This process results in fairer premiums and better coverage tailored to your needs.

## Honesty is Crucial

It might be tempting to withhold information, but full disclosure is essential. Insurers have ways to verify your medical history, and non-disclosure can lead to denied claims. Always be honest during underwriting. If a medical professional knows something, the insurers can find out.

## Claiming Made Easy

Underwritten policies are generally easier to claim against because the insurer has already assessed the risk upfront. The typical process involves notifying the insurer, providing necessary documentation, and then receiving the payout if the claim is valid.

## Striving for Self-Insurance

As I advise my clients, my goal is to help you become fully self-insured. Achieving financial independence to where you no longer rely on insurance is the ultimate protection. This is done by having enough wealth in financial capital to cover any needs you might have and sustain your living standard in the event of injury or illness.

By understanding and implementing these protections, you can secure your financial future, provide for your loved ones, and ensure peace of mind. Remember, personal protection is not just about today; it's about shielding your tomorrow.

# CHAPTER 6

# BUILDING WEALTH WITH OR WITHOUT STRATEGIC DEBT - SMART MOVES FOR FINANCIAL GROWTH

# STRATEGY 6.1 –
# INVESTING FOR A GOAL

## How to Invest for a Goal

Investing for a specific goal requires a clear understanding of the timeframe, the risk you can tolerate, and a consistent approach. Timeframes play a crucial role in determining the level of risk you should take. For simplicity, we have ignored taxes in these examples, as they are generally minimal when starting with small regular contributions rather than a lump sum. Here, we will explore how to invest for a house, an improved lifestyle, and for your children's future, taking into account the different time horizons and investment strategies.

## Investing for a House Outside Super

When saving for a house outside of superannuation, the timeframe is vital. If you are saving for a first or second house and want to build up funds within a certain period, it's important to balance risk and return. You are limited as to how much you can put in your super for your first house, so if you are buying a second house or even your first, you need to save some funds outside super. The shorter the time frame, the less risk you should take to reduce the risk of losing money.

### Example: Saving for a Second House in 7 Years

**Goal:** Save $100,000 in 7 years

**Expected Return:** 7% per annum (growth portfolio - 70% to 80% in growth assets vs income/defensive assets)

**Monthly Contribution:** Approximately $999.43

To reach your goal of $100,000 in 7 years with an average annual return of 7%, you would need to invest approximately $999.43 per month.

The total tax paid over 7 years, assuming a 30% tax rate on the returns from the investment, would be approximately $7,051.97.

## Investing for Lifestyle in 5 Years

If you have a mortgage on your house and would like to save for a better life, it is generally worth saving in the offset account or paying directly into the mortgage. The only difference is that saving directly into the mortgage means the bank can decide to hold the funds if the value of the property goes down, but this rarely happens. If you don't have a mortgage and want to save for an improved lifestyle, investing in a diversified portfolio can be a good approach.

### Example: Saving for an Improved Lifestyle in 5 Years

**Goal:** Save $100,000 in 5 years to withdraw $7,000 annually for an improved lifestyle

**Expected Return:** 5% per annum

**Monthly Contribution:** Approximately $1,471.35 pm

To reach your goal of $100,000 in 5 years with an average annual return of 5%, you would need to invest approximately $1,471.35 per month.

Why even bother if you are saving 18k a year already? It builds a great habit and you can actually use these savings for other goals. I have worked with clients at various life stages and I can assure you that your goals will change over time, and this is a great habit to have for a fulfilling life.

# Investing for Kids for 25 Years

Investing for your children's future is one of the most rewarding financial goals. Parents should generally not use bank accounts or normal investment accounts for this purpose; instead, use educational bonds or investment growth bonds. These bonds offer tax advantages and structured growth, making them ideal for long-term savings.

**Benefits of Growth Bonds**

- **Tax Efficiency:** Growth bonds can offer tax advantages, as earnings are often tax-deferred until maturity or withdrawal. Generally if held for longer than 10 years, you nor the future beneficiary don't pay any taxes in your personal name once you start accessing the funds.

- **Flexibility:** They can be used for a variety of purposes, such as education, buying a house, or starting a business.

- **Structured Growth:** These bonds provide a disciplined approach to saving and investing, ensuring consistent contributions and compounding growth over time.

- **Transferability:** Growth bonds are amazing as well because they can be easily transferred without any capital gains implications. This means if little John becomes a naughty kid, you don't have to give the money to him.

- **Control:** It provides you with control even if you pass away. I always tell grandparents, this helps you still rule from the grave if needed for naughty Jane. This is because you can lay down specific estate planning instructions around the account. For example, you want the funds to be given to Jane when she is 27 and based on XYZ or, she can only take 5% every year, etc.

**Example: Investing for a Child's Future Over 25 Years**

**Goal:** Invest $100 every fortnight for a 2-year-old until they are 27 years old

**Expected Return:** 10% per annum

**Total Contributions:** $65,000

**Final Amount:** Approximately $289,229

By investing $100 every fortnight (totalling $65,000 over 25 years) with an average annual return of 10%, you would accumulate approximately $289,229 by the time the child is 27 years old.

## Conclusion

Investing for specific goals requires a strategic approach that takes into account the time frame, risk tolerance, and consistent contributions. Whether saving for a house, an improved lifestyle, or your children's future, understanding how much to invest regularly and choosing the right investment vehicles are key to achieving your financial objectives. Remember, the longer the time frame, the more risk you should be willing to take, potentially leading to higher returns.

Always review and adjust your investment strategy as needed to stay on track toward your goals.

# STRATEGY 6.2 – LEVERAGE SMART DEBT TO BUILD WEALTH

## Introduction: Debt as a Tool for Wealth Creation

Debt often carries a negative connotation, but when used strategically, it can be a powerful tool for building wealth. In this section, we'll explore the concepts of bad debt, good debt, and smart debt, and demonstrate how leveraging debt can enhance your investment returns. We'll use a real-world scenario to illustrate the potential benefits and risks.

## Understanding Bad, Good, and Smart Debt

### Bad Debt

**Definition:** Debt that depletes your wealth and offers no potential for return.

Examples:

- **Personal Credit Card Debt:** High interest rates and no asset creation.

- **Personal Loans for Consumables:** Loans for items like vacations or luxury goods that do not appreciate in value.

# Good Debt

**Definition:** Debt that helps you acquire assets that appreciate in value.

Examples:

- **Principal Place of Residence Mortgage Loans:** For purchasing property you live in and that appreciates in value.

- **Student Loans:** Investing in education that increases your earning potential. This is a tricky one, as if this debt doesn't increase your earning potential, it is a bad debt. So be very strategic with student debts.

# Smart Debt

**Definition:** Debt used strategically to leverage investments, maximising returns while managing risks. These also have to be tax deductible.

Examples:

- **Margin Loans:** Borrowing to invest in diversified funds or stocks.

- **Investment Mortgage Loans:** For purchasing property you rent out and that appreciates in value. Note, if this property is not generating income at the time, it might not be tax deductible.

- **Business Loans:** Financing that drives business growth and revenue.

The higher your margin tax rate, the larger benefit you get from using smart debt. Generally, for those that can stomach the movements in the market, you should use as much of this to build wealth until you retire.

## Case Study: Leveraging Debt for Investment

Let's illustrate smart debt with an example of investing in a diversified fund using borrowed money.

### Scenario Details

- **Initial Investment:** $10,000 (50% debt, 50% equity)
- **Monthly Investment:** $400 (50% debt, 50% equity)
- **Debt Amount:** $5,000 initial, $200 per month
- **Investment Fund:** Vanguard High Growth Fund and we will use an 8% return (lower end of long term performance)

### Debt Rates

- **CommSec:** 5.5%
- **BT:** 6.0%
- **Provider 3:** 5.8%
- **Average Debt Rate:** 5.77%

### Investment Performance

Using historical data from the Vanguard High Growth Fund, we'll model the investment performance from 2004 to 2024 (20 years).

### Final Results in 2024

- **Final Investment Value:** $275,232.58
- **Initial Total Contribution Value:** $53,000 (from pocket)
- **Initial Total Contribution Value from debt:** $53,000 (from pocket)
- **Final Net Value:** $222,232.58

### Approximate Interest and Tax Deduction

- **Total Interest Paid:** $39,092
- **Total Tax Deduction:** $11,727

# Risks and Considerations

## Risks

1. **Market Volatility:** Investment values can fluctuate, leading to potential losses.

2. **Interest Rates:** Rising interest rates increase the cost of borrowing.

3. **Margin Calls:** If the value of the investment falls significantly, you may need to add more funds to maintain the loan.

## Managing Risks

- **Diversification:** Spread investments across various assets to reduce risk.

- **Regular Monitoring:** Keep track of investment performance and adjust strategies as needed.

- **Limit Borrowing:** Only borrow amounts you can manage and repay comfortably. In the example a 50% borrowing was used.

# Setting Up Your Investment Account

## Steps to Get Started

1. **Choose a Broker:** Select a brokerage firm that offers margin loans.

2. **Open an Account:** Complete the necessary paperwork to open an investment account.

3. **Apply for a Margin Loan:** Submit an application for the margin loan, specifying the amount you intend to borrow. You don't need to use the full credit amount you are given.

4. **Select Investments:** Choose a diversified fund that can provide a return higher than the margin loan. This ensures you are moving forward and not backwards.

5. **Monitor and Adjust:** Regularly review your investment portfolio and make adjustments as needed.

## The Power of Diversification

Diversification is crucial in managing investment risk. By spreading your investments across different asset classes, you can mitigate the impact of any single investment's poor performance. As highlighted in previous chapters, a diversified portfolio is key to long-term financial success.

## Conclusion

Using debt strategically can significantly enhance your wealth-building efforts. By understanding the differences between bad, good, and smart debt, and by leveraging borrowed funds wisely, you can maximise your investment returns. Always remember to diversify, monitor your investments, and manage risks to achieve your financial goals.

# CHAPTER 7

# SUPER AND RETIREMENT – CONSISTENT STRATEGIES FOR A SECURE FUTURE

# STRATEGY 7 – REGULARLY REVISIT YOUR SUPER FOR OPTIMAL OUTCOMES

Building a secure retirement requires consistent and strategic actions throughout your working life. This chapter will explore how to leverage your superannuation effectively at different stages leading up to and during retirement, using strategies that maximise your financial security and quality of life.

## Accumulation and Super in the Younger Years (35 Years Before Retirement)

### Leveraging Super for a First Home

One of the significant advantages of superannuation is the ability to use it to buy your first home through the First Home Super Saver Scheme (FHSSS). This scheme allows you to make voluntary super contributions to save for your first home, benefiting from the concessional tax treatment of superannuation. I reckon it is a must for people who want to buy their first home to live in.

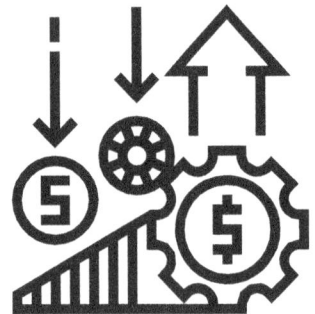

# First Home Super Saver Scheme (FHSSS)

**Concept:** The FHSSS allows individuals to save money for their first home inside their super fund, benefiting from the concessional tax treatment of superannuation.

**Steps to Use the FHSSS**

1. **Make Voluntary Contributions:**
   - **Annual Cap:** You can contribute up to $15,000 per year.
   - **Total Cap:** The maximum amount you can contribute under the scheme is $50,000.
   - **Type of Contributions:** These contributions can be either concessional (before-tax) or non-concessional (after-tax).

2. **Request a Release:**
   - **Eligibility:** Once you're ready to buy a home, you can apply to the Australian Taxation Office (ATO) to release the voluntary contributions along with the associated earnings.
   - **Process:** The ATO will assess your application, determine the amount that can be released, and instruct your super fund to release the funds to you.

3. **Use the Funds:**
   - **Deposit:** The released funds must be used towards your first owner occupied purchase.
   - **Timeline:** You must sign a contract to purchase or construct your first home within 12 months of receiving the FHSSS amount, although you can apply for an extension of a further 12 months.

**Example:** Let's look at a fictitious example of how the FHSSS can be used effectively.

**Profile**
- **Age:** 25
- **Monthly Contribution:** $833.33

**Duration**
- **Period:** 5 years
  Doing this a long time before you need the funds is key to success.

**Calculations:**

1. **Total Contributions:** Total Contributions = $833.33 × 12 × 5 = $50,000

2. Total tax saved by these contributions - on a salary of $80,000, you would save $3,200 per annum in taxes roughly if you contribute $10,000 into your super for this on a concessional level.

3. **Assumed Earnings:**
   - Let's assume an annual return of 7.34% within the super fund.
   - This is also guaranteed by the government but it is reviewed every quarter. It is called the SIC (shortfall interest charge rates).

4. **Future Value of Contributions:** I won't bore you with this but you can use any of these calculators to see what it will look like:
   - https://rest.com.au/tools-advice/tools/calculators/first-home

5. **Estimated Total Available:** Including the initial contributions and the earnings, the total amount available could be around $49,993. If the money had been saved in a normal bank account, it would end up at around $38,429 (based on 4.5% outside super returns on a term deposit).

Using the FHSSS, a 25-year-old making consistent monthly contributions of $833.33 over 5 years can accumulate approximately $49,993 (including taxes saved every year, if no return is gotten on the taxes saved, you will have saved $65,993), including earnings at a 7.34% annual return rate. This amount can significantly aid in making a home deposit, leveraging the tax benefits and concessional treatment of superannuation to reach your home ownership goal faster. This example illustrates how contributions can grow over time, providing a substantial amount towards purchasing your first home. If you are a couple, you will have about $134k towards your deposit.

## Impact of Changing to Lower Fees in a Diversified Fund

Reducing fees and optimising returns can significantly impact your retirement savings. Fees can eat away at your returns, so choosing a fund with lower fees but maintaining a good return rate is essential.

Example:
- **Age:** 30
- **Starting Balance:** $82,000

- **Employer Contributions:** $12,000 annually, increasing with 3% inflation.

**Scenario 1: Higher return fund at 10% p.a. with standard fees.**
**Scenario 2: Lower fees by 0.5% but a 7% return.**

**Calculation:**

**Higher Return Fund (10%):**

- **Future Value after 35 years:** Approximately $3,016,714

**Lower Fees Fund (7%):**

- **Future Value after 35 years:** Approximately $1,474,351

It's not just about the lowest fees; the return on investment (asset allocation) matters significantly. Opting for a slightly higher fee with better returns can drastically increase your retirement savings.

## Impact of Changing Funds for Slightly Better Returns

Switching to a fund with a slightly better return can have a dramatic effect on your retirement savings.

Example:
- **Age:** 30
- **Starting Balance:** $82,000
- **Employer Contributions:** $12,000 annually, increasing with 3% inflation.

**Scenario 1: Switching to a fund with a 10% return per annum.**
**Scenario 2: Remaining in a fund with a 9% return per annum.**

**Calculation:**

**Higher Return Fund (10%):**

- **Future Value after 35 years (At age 65):** Approximately $3,016,714

**Lower Return Fund (9%):**

- **Future Value after 35 years:** Approximately $2,484,368

**Difference:** The higher return fund results in an additional $532,346 over 35 years.

Switching to a higher-performing fund with slightly better returns can significantly increase your retirement savings over the long term.

Future Value after 35 years (At age 65)

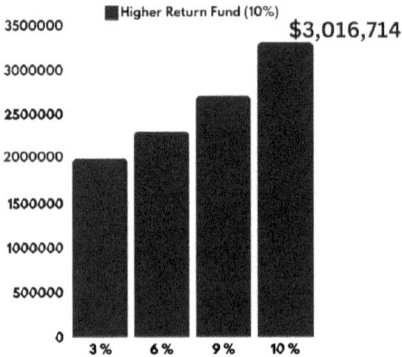

Higher Return Fund (10%)

$3,016,714

Future Value after 35 years

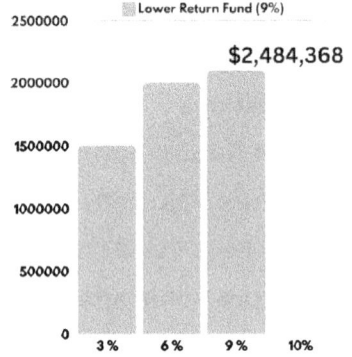

Lower Return Fund (9%)

$2,484,368

**Difference: $532,346 over 35 years**

## The Importance of Consistency

Consistent contributions and monitoring of your superannuation can lead to substantial growth over time. Regularly review your super fund's performance and make adjustments as necessary to ensure you are on track to meet your retirement goals. What we see in the advice industry is, new, better and cheaper products are put on the market every year, so it is worth reviewing this on a consistent basis to get a cheaper fund and potentially higher returns but in the right asset allocation.

Moving in and out of different investment options due to change in the market conditions, especially driven by fear or greed, will lead to lower performance returns over time. You want to remain diversified and in the right investment option but just make other tweaks as needed.

## Pre/Transition-Retirement (5 Years Before Retirement)

### Maximising Super Contributions

Five years before retirement, it's crucial to move as many assets into superannuation as possible. This is because, in the

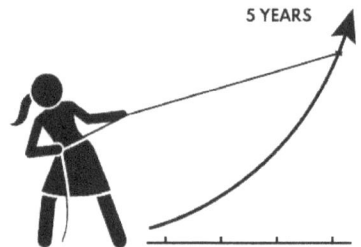

retirement phase, earnings on super balances below $1.9 million are not taxed. This cap is known as the transfer balance cap. We will explore just normal contributions to super or doing it through a transition to retirement strategy.

# Transition to Retirement

Transition to Retirement (TTR) is a strategy designed to help individuals who are approaching retirement age to ease into retirement while potentially boosting their superannuation savings and reducing their tax liabilities. This section will explain how TTR works and provide an example of how someone earning $90,000 annually plus superannuation at 12% can utilise this strategy for tax savings and superannuation growth. This strategy works best for people who don't have surplus cash flow but would like to save some taxes and boost their superannuation accounts.

## Understanding Transition to Retirement (TTR)

**What is TTR?** TTR allows individuals aged 55 and over (depending on when you were born) to access a portion of their superannuation while still working. The primary objectives of a TTR strategy are to:

- Supplement income if reducing work hours.
- Boost superannuation savings through salary sacrificing.
- Potentially reduce tax liabilities.

**Key Features of TTR:**

1. **Access to Superannuation:** You can draw down a portion of your super as an income stream (between 4% and 10% of the super balance per year).
2. **Continued Contributions:** Continue to work and contribute to your super within the limits.
3. **Tax Efficiency:** Potentially reduce your taxable income and increase superannuation savings.

**Example Scenario: John's Transition to Retirement**

**Name:** John

**Age:** 58

**Annual Income:** $90,000

**Superannuation Guarantee (SG):** 12% of salary ($10,800 annually)

**Scenario 1: John Needs Extra Cash Flow**

**John's Objective:** Supplement his income without reducing work hours.

1. **Start a TTR Pension:** John starts a TTR pension, drawing down 4% of his superannuation balance annually. Assuming his super balance is $300,000:

   ○ **Annual Pension Payment:** 4% of $300,000 = $12,000

2. **Tax Treatment:**

   ○ **Taxable Component:** $10,000
   ○ **Tax-Free Component:** $2,000
   ○ **Marginal Tax Rate:** 30%
   ○ **Tax Offset:** 15% on the taxable component

**Tax on Taxable Component:**
Tax on Taxable Component = $10,000 × 0.30 = $3,000
Tax Offset = $10,000 × 0.15 = $1,500
Net Tax on Taxable Component = $3,000 – $1,500 = $1,500

**Total Tax:**
Tax on Tax-Free Component = $0
Total Tax = $1,500

**Net Pension Income:**
Net Pension Income = $12,000 – $1,500 = $10,500

**Total Income with TTR Pension**

1. **Salary:** $70,800

2. **Salary Sacrificed:** $19,200

3. **Tax on Salary:**

   ○ **Taxable Salary:** $70,800
   ○ **Marginal Tax Rate Calculation:**
   $70,800 (2024-2025 tax year)
   Tax = $14,248

4. **Net Salary:** Net Salary = $70,800 – $14,248 = $56,552

**Total Net Income with TTR Pension:** Total Net Income = Net Salary + Net Pension = $56,552 + $10,500 = $67,052

Without TTR total net income would have been = $69,608 per annum.

**Key Benefits:**

1. Taxes saved - $6,144 (tax paid on 90k Income vs that on 70.8k income). This can supplement income.

2. Increased super balance by - $16,320 (this is the net value as tax paid in super on the $19,200 contributed).

3. Reduced taxes on the earnings of the fund inside his super.

**Scenario 2: John Does Not Need Extra Cash Flow and Wants to Maximise Superannuation**

**John's Objective:** Boost his super savings and reduce taxable income.

1. **Salary Sacrifice:** John decides to salary sacrifice an additional $19,200 into his superannuation each year. This keeps him within the concessional contributions cap ($30,000 including the SG contributions).

   - **Salary Sacrificed:** $19,200

   - **SG Contributions:** $10,800

   - **Total Concessional Contributions:** $30,000 (cap limit)

2. **Tax Implications:**

   - **Salary Sacrificed Amount:** This amount is taxed at 15% within the super fund instead of John's marginal tax rate (likely 30%).

   - **Tax Saving:**

     - Without Salary Sacrifice: $19,200 taxed at 30% = $5,760

     - With Salary Sacrifice: $19,200 taxed at 15% = $2,880

     - **Tax Saving:** $5,760 - $2,880 = $2,880

3. **New Income Structure:**

   - **Gross Salary:** $90,000

   - **Less Salary Sacrifice:** $19,200

   - **Taxable Income:** $70,800

4. **Tax on Salary:**

   - **Marginal Tax Rate Calculation:**
     $70,800 (2024-2024 tax year)
     Tax Calculation = $14,248

5. **Net Salary:** Net Salary = $70,800 − $14,248 = $56,552

6. **Total Net Income:** Total Net Income = Net Salary = $56,552

7. **Superannuation Growth:**
   ◦ **Contributions:**
     ▪ SG: $10,800
     ▪ Salary Sacrifice: $19,200
     ▪ Total Annual Contributions: $30,000
   ◦ **Compounded Growth:** Assuming a conservative growth rate of 5% annually, John's super balance will grow significantly over the years leading to retirement by an extra $129,882.31 after taxes.

## Additional Considerations

1. **Contribution Caps:** Ensure concessional contributions do not exceed the annual cap of $30,000 to avoid additional tax penalties.

2. **Age Pension Eligibility:** Understand how TTR and increased super balances might affect eligibility for the age pension.

3. **Personal and Family Impact:** Discuss with family members to ensure the TTR strategy aligns with overall financial goals and lifestyle.

4. **Financial Advice:** Seek advice from a financial planner to tailor the TTR strategy to individual circumstances and maximise benefits. I am only scratching the surface as to how we help!'

Transition to retirement strategies can be a powerful tool for those approaching retirement age. By utilising salary sacrifice and accessing superannuation income streams, individuals like John can manage their tax liabilities efficiently while growing their superannuation balance. Whether supplementing income or boosting retirement savings, TTR offers flexibility and financial benefits that align with long-term retirement goals.

# Retirement Years

## Managing Longevity and Income

**Longevity:** Ensuring your funds last through retirement is critical. Investing in a diversified portfolio helps manage risk while providing growth potential. As you near retirement, it's important to shift your asset allocation to reduce risk.

**Age Pension:** If eligible, the age pension can supplement your income. However, aiming to be a self-funded retiree provides more financial security and independence.

## Investment Strategy:

- **Reduce Risk:** Shift towards lower-risk investments but maintain diversification.

- **Funds vs. Term Deposits:** Managed funds often provide better returns than term deposits and come with professional management.

**Example:** Assume you have a diversified portfolio that includes a mix of equities, bonds, and cash equivalents. Over time, you would adjust this mix to reduce exposure to high-risk assets while ensuring enough growth to outpace inflation.

This example is to illustrate how taking funds from super to fund retirement needs to be carefully planned and managed over time to ensure you have enough in your latter years and don't run out of money.

**Scenario 1:**

**Name:** John and Mary

**Combined Superannuation Balance:** $1,200,000
*Note to younger clients - The equivalent value of $1,200,000 in 30 years for a 37 year old who will be 67 then, is $3,892,080. So when planning, do think of things in today's value regardless of your age.*

**Age:** 67

**Annual Withdrawal:** $120,000

**Expected Return on Superannuation:** 6% annually after all fees

**Life Expectancy:** Based on Mary's longer life expectancy (let's assume 20 years for this calculation).

### Pension Eligibility

Assuming John and Mary are eligible for the Age Pension, the amount they receive will depend on their combined assets and income. For simplicity, let's estimate the potential pension they might receive based on their superannuation balance at the given points in time. Let us assume this is a plus for them, so they don't really care about it but will apply to spend on extra holidays or to give this to charity, kids or grandkids.

### Superannuation Balances and Potential Pension

| Year | Balance ($) | Approximate Annual Pension ($) |
|------|-------------|-------------------------------|
| 5 | 929,419 | 17,000 |
| 10 | 786,029 | 22,000 |
| 20 | 294,257 | 34,000 |

### Notes on Pension Estimates

1. **Year 5 Balance:** With a balance of $929,419, John and Mary are likely to receive a partial pension. The estimated annual pension is around $17,000.

2. **Year 10 Balance:** With a balance of $786,029, they might receive a slightly higher partial pension, estimated at $22,000 annually.

3. **Year 20 Balance:** With a balance of $294,257, they are likely to receive a near full pension, estimated at $34,000 annually.

### Conclusion

John and Mary, with a combined superannuation balance of $1.2 million, can withdraw $120,000 annually. After 5 years, their balance will be approximately $929,419; after 10 years, it will be around $786,029; and by the 20th year (Mary's life expectancy), their balance would be about $294,257.

Additionally, they will be eligible for the Age Pension, which will help supplement their income. By the 5th year, they might receive around $17,000 annually from the pension; by the 10th year, around $22,000 annually; and by the 20th year, around $34,000 annually. This scenario highlights the importance of combining superannuation withdrawals with potential pension benefits to ensure financial sustainability throughout retirement. If they withdrew $130,000 instead every year, they would run out of money by the 13th year. This extra 10k puts a huge dent into their retirement plans and leads to longevity risk.

## Staying Connected and Active

**Social Engagement:** Staying active through volunteering or part-time work can enhance your quality of life in retirement. It provides a sense of purpose and keeps you connected with the community.

**Balancing Responsibilities:** Many retirees face the dual challenges of supporting ageing parents and assisting their children. Balancing these responsibilities requires careful financial planning.

**Example:** A retiree who volunteers at a local community centre or works part-time at a library can maintain social connections and mental stimulation, contributing to overall well-being.

## Superannuation as Your Largest Asset

Even if your super exceeds the $1.9 million cap, the earnings of anything above this amount are taxed at 15%, which is still favourable compared to personal tax rates. So super is your biggest asset that should be cherished and really utilised. The government and authorities will never make it tax ineffective to put money into super but they will consistently change the limits. So worry less about the government but what benefits you can use now and in the future.

## Conclusion

Superannuation should be the cornerstone of your retirement planning. Consistent contributions, strategic asset allocation, and thoughtful planning can ensure a comfortable and secure retirement. By leveraging super effectively, you can maximise your savings, minimise tax liabilities, and provide yourself with a fulfilling retirement.

# Aged Care Years

As we age, planning for aged care becomes an essential aspect of our financial and personal planning. Aged care can encompass a range of services, from in-home support to full residential care. Understanding what to expect, how to plan for it, and the different entry requirements based on financial means is crucial for ensuring a comfortable and secure future.

## What to Expect

**Types of Aged Care Services:**

1. **Home Care:** Services provided in your home, such as cleaning, cooking, and personal care.

2. **Residential Care:** Full-time care in a facility, offering accommodation, meals, personal care, and health services.

3. **Respite Care:** Short-term care to give regular carers a break.

4. **Palliative Care:** Specialised care for those with serious illnesses, focusing on comfort and quality of life.

**Costs Involved:**

- **Home Care:** Costs can vary based on the level of support needed. Government subsidies are available through programs like the Commonwealth Home Support Programme (CHSP) and Home Care Packages (HCP).

- **Residential Care:** Includes accommodation fees, daily care fees, and additional service fees. Government subsidies are also available, but means testing will determine your contribution.

## Planning for Aged Care

**Start Early:**

- **Financial Planning:** Begin considering aged care options early in your retirement planning. This ensures you have the necessary funds and can make informed decisions.

- **Health Care Directives:** Have clear directives and a power of attorney in place to make decisions if you are unable to do so.

**Assess Your Needs:**

- **Health Needs:** Evaluate your current and potential future health needs.

- **Financial Situation:** Assess your financial assets, including savings, superannuation, and potential home equity.

**Research Options:**

- **Aged Care Facilities:** Visit facilities, talk to staff, and understand the services and costs.

- **Government Support:** Investigate government programs and subsidies that can help offset costs.

# Entry Requirements

### Low Means Entry

For those with limited financial assets:

- **Means Testing:** Your income and assets will be assessed to determine your ability to contribute to the cost of care. If very minimal, you can go in as a low means resident.

- **Government Support:** Significant government support is available to cover the majority of costs, but you may still need to contribute a portion based on your means. This includes the Basic Daily Fee, which all residents pay.

- **Cost Range:** Typically, you might expect to pay around $61.96 per day for the Basic Daily Fee, with other fees heavily subsidised.

### Normal Entry

For those with moderate financial means:

- **Means Testing:** You will undergo means testing, which may result in higher contributions compared to low means entry.

- **Accommodation Payment:** You may need to pay a Refundable Accommodation Deposit (RAD) or a Daily Accommodation Payment (DAP), which can be negotiated based on your financial situation.

- **Basic Daily Fee:** As of current rates, this fee is approximately $61.96 per day. All residents in aged care facilities are required to pay a Basic Daily Fee, which contributes to day-to-day living costs such as meals, laundry, and cleaning.

- **Additional Services:** You may opt for extra services, such as a higher standard of accommodation or additional activities, which incur extra fees.

- **Cost Range:** The RAD can range from $300,000 to $1 million, while the DAP can range from $50 to $200 per day depending on RAD.

## High Net Worth

For those with substantial financial assets:

- **Full Payment:** You may be expected to pay the full cost of aged care services, including accommodation and additional services.

- **Investment Considerations:** Consider how your assets can be structured to fund your care without significantly impacting your estate planning.

- **Tailored Services:** High net worth individuals can access more luxurious and personalised care options, ensuring the highest level of comfort and support.

- **Basic Daily Fee:** As of current rates, this fee is approximately $61.96 per day. All residents in aged care facilities are required to pay a Basic Daily Fee, which contributes to day-to-day living costs such as meals, laundry, and cleaning.

- **Cost Range:** Full payment for high-end aged care can exceed $1 million for RAD and additional daily costs ranging from $200 to $500 per day for premium services.

Planning for aged care is a critical part of retirement planning that requires careful consideration of your health needs and financial situation. Whether you have low means, moderate financial assets, or substantial wealth, understanding the options and costs associated with aged care will help you make informed decisions and ensure a secure and comfortable future. Each situation is unique, and consulting with financial planners and aged care specialists can provide tailored advice to suit your specific needs and circumstances.

# BONUS CHAPTER:

# HOW TO BUILD A MILLION DOLLARS IN ASSETS IN 15 YEARS ON AN AVERAGE WAGE

# BONUS CHAPTER

Building material wealth within a decade and a half is achievable even on an average income. This chapter will outline a strategic plan for someone earning $105,000 annually to increase their wealth from $140,000 to over $1 million. By leveraging investments, property, and strategic (smart) debt, you can achieve substantial growth in your assets. Additionally, factoring in the tax benefits and potentially reinvesting them into the investment account can maximise growth.

## Step 1: Initial Financial Snapshot

**Current Financial Position:**

- **Income:** $105,000 annually
- **Initial Savings:** $140,000

## Step 2: Investment Property Strategy

**Property Purchase:**

- **Investment Property Value:** $500,000
- **Bank Loan:** $400,000 (Interest-only mortgage at 6%)
- **Down Payment:** $100,000 (from initial savings)

**Property Growth:**

- **Capital Growth Rate:** 3.5% annually

- **Rental Yield:** 4.5% of the property value annually

**Annual Property Income:**

- **Rental Income:** $22,500 (initially)

- **Interest on Loan:** $24,000 annually

- **Net Rental Income:** Rental Income - Interest Payment

## Step 3: Diversified Fund Investment

### Initial Investment:

- **Amount:** $30,000 (from initial savings)

### Ongoing Contributions:

- **Personal Contribution:** $975 per month

- **Borrowed Contribution:** $975 per month (at 7% interest rate)

### Investment Returns:

- **Return Rate:** 8% annually

- **Annual Contribution:** $23,400

# Detailed Calculations

*If you don't like math, close your eyes ... well just skip to the 'final wealth' section below.*

### Property Investment:

### Annual Capital Growth:
Future Value = Initial Value × (1 + Growth Rate)^ Years
Future Value = $500,000 × (1 + 0.035)^15 ≈ $837,674

### Rental Income:
Annual Rental Income = Initial Rental Yield × Property Value
Net Rental Income = Annual Rental Income – Interest Payment

Net Rental Income (Year 1) = $22,500 – $24,000 = –$1,500
(Note: Net rental income should improve over time due to increasing property value and rental income.)

**Diversified Fund Investment:**

**Future Value of Monthly Contributions:**

$FV = P \times ((((1 + r)^n) - 1)/r)$

Where:

- P is the monthly contribution ($1,950)

- r is the monthly return rate (0.67%) (monthly interest)

- n is the total number of contributions (180 as 15 years by 12 months)

**Calculation:**

**Future Value of Monthly Contributions:**

$FV = (1950) \times ((((1+0.08/12)^{180}) - 1)/0.0067)$

$FV \approx 1950 \times 347.27 \approx$

$FV \approx 677,171$

**Adding Initial Investment Growth:**

Total Future Value = $677,171 + (30,000 \times (1+0.08)^{15})$

Total Future Value = $677,171 + 95,165.07$

Total Future Value $\approx 772,336.07$

Less Debt Owed = 772,336.07 - 175,500 = 596,836.07

**Including Tax Benefits**

**Interest on Margin Loan:**

Annual Interest Payment = $975 \times 12 \times 0.0712 = \$819$

**Tax Deduction:**

Tax Deduction = Annual Interest Payment × Marginal Tax Rate

Tax Deduction = $\$819 \times 0.30 \approx \$245.70$

**Reinvested Tax Benefit:**

We'll assume the tax benefit is reinvested annually. For simplicity, we won't compound it, but it can be added as a lump sum contribution each year.

# Final Wealth Calculation

## Property Wealth After 15 Years:

- **Property Value:** $837,674

- **Mortgage Remaining:** $400,000 (interest-only loan)

- **Equity in Property:** $437,674

## Total Wealth After 15 Years:
Total Wealth = Equity in Property + Investment Portfolio Value

Total Wealth = $437,674 + 596,836.07 ≈ $1,034,510

# Incorporating Negative Cash Flow and Tax Benefits

We need to account for the negative cash flow and tax benefits each year over the 15-year period. Assuming the net rental income improves linearly, and tax benefits are reinvested:

**Total Negative Cash Flow (simplified):**
Total Negative Cash Flow = –1,500×15 ≈ –22,500

**Total Reinvested Tax Benefits:**
Total Tax Benefits = $245.70 × 15 ≈ $3,685.50

Adjusting the final wealth to account for these:

## Adjusted Investment Portfolio Value:

Adjusted Portfolio Value = 596,836.07 – 22,500 + 3,685.50 = $578,021

*For simplicity, I have excluded property depreciation and other tax benefits. We model these details for clients, but they are unnecessary for this simple demonstration.*

## Final Total Wealth:
Total Wealth = Equity in Property + Adjusted Portfolio Value
Total Wealth = $437,674 + $578,021
Total Wealth = $1,015,695

# Risks and Considerations

## Market Volatility

**Description:** Investments in property and diversified funds are subject to market fluctuations. The value of these investments can rise and fall, sometimes significantly, over short periods.

**Management:**

- **Diversification:** Spread investments across different asset classes to reduce risk.
- **Long-Term Perspective:** Focus on long-term goals rather than short-term market movements.

## Interest Rates - Understanding This Stabilising

**Description:** Changes in interest rates can affect loan repayments and investment returns. Higher interest rates increase borrowing costs, while lower rates may reduce returns on fixed-income investments but increase returns on growth assets. The economics behind interest rates is very interesting and a way to think about it, is the long term return on assets, especially a diversified portfolio, will always be more that interest rates. Interest rate is a monetary policy tool used to stabilise the economy, so it is working in your favour over a long period of time.

**Management:**

- **Fixed-Rate Loans:** Consider locking in interest rates on loans to manage repayment costs. I don't like it as it defeats the purpose of going with the flow of this stabilising tool. However, it can be a peace of mind approach (psychological benefit)
- **Flexible Strategies:** Be prepared to change providers if you can find a cheaper rate, it is tax deductible, not a tax offset, so you want cheaper rates if you can find it.

# Debt Management

**Description:** High levels of debt can be risky if not managed properly. This includes the potential for margin calls if the value of leveraged investments falls. You need to always be within your means with debt and ensure you start small to understand it before fully going in.

**Management:**

- **Debt Ratios:** Monitor and maintain healthy debt-to-equity ratios. In the example above, we only used a 50% debt to equity ratio, so it is a huge buffer to reduce any margin calls you might have.

- **Emergency Fund:** Keep a reserve of funds to cover unexpected expenses or margin calls.

# Tax Benefits

**Description:** While tax deductions can enhance returns, they depend on consistent income and stable tax regulations. Changes in tax laws could affect the benefits of this strategy.

**Management:**

- **Tax Planning:** Work with a tax advisor to optimise and adapt your strategy as needed.

- **Compliance:** Ensure all investments and deductions comply with current tax laws.

# Steps to Implement the Strategy

## 1. Property Purchase:

- **Secure Financing:** Work with a mortgage broker to obtain a loan.
- **Find a Property:** Choose a property with good growth potential and rental yield.
- **Purchase and Manage:** Buy the property and manage it, either personally or through a property manager (use comparative advantage).

## 2. Diversified Fund Investment:

- **Open an Account:** Choose a reputable brokerage or investment platform.
- **Set Up Contributions:** Automate monthly contributions from both personal and borrowed funds.
- **Monitor Performance:** Regularly review the performance of your investments.

## 3. Tax Benefits:

- **Calculate Deductions:** Track interest payments on borrowed funds.
- **Reinvest Benefits:** Reinvest tax deductions annually to maximise growth.

## 4. Regular Reviews:

- **Performance Monitoring:** Regularly check the performance of both property and investment portfolios.
- **Adjust Strategy:** Make necessary adjustments to stay on track with financial goals.

# Other Considerations

### Financial Goals:

- Clarify the purpose of your wealth-building strategy. Are you saving for retirement, funding your children's education, or planning for a major purchase? Clear goals will help guide your investment decisions.

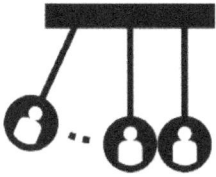

### Lifestyle Impact:

- **Balance:** Ensure that your strategy allows you to enjoy life. Investing heavily should not come at the expense of your current quality of life. Maintain a balance between saving and spending.

- **Family Involvement:** Discuss the plan with your partner and family. Their support and understanding are crucial. Consider how the strategy might impact your family's lifestyle and future plans.

### Long-term Sustainability:

- **Reassessment:** Reevaluate your strategy periodically to ensure it aligns with your changing life circumstances and financial goals.

- **Flexibility:** Be prepared to adjust your approach as needed. Economic conditions, personal circumstances, and goals can change over time.

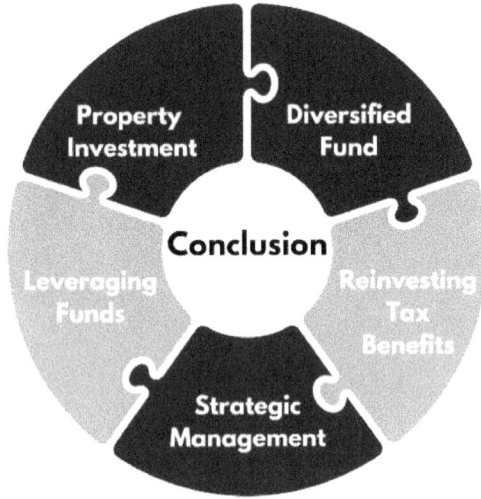

## Conclusion

Using a combination of property investment and a diversified fund, leveraging both personal and borrowed funds, and reinvesting tax benefits can significantly increase wealth. By strategically managing investments and consistently contributing, achieving substantial financial growth within 15 years is highly attainable. This strategic approach ensures that you can make the most of your resources and achieve your financial goals efficiently while considering the broader impact on your lifestyle and family.

# References

**References Summary**

**Books and Articles**

1. **CFA Institute:**
   - *Behavioural Finance.* Retrieved from CFA Institute
   - This source helped in understanding the classification of biases into emotional and cognitive.

**Financial Data and Tools**

2. **Canstar:**
   - *Life Insurance Ratings.* Retrieved from Canstar Life Insurance Ratings
   - Provides ratings for life insurance policies in Australia.

3. **Finder:**
   - *Best Life Insurance.* Retrieved from Finder Life Insurance Ratings
   - Offers detailed reviews and ratings of life insurance policies.

4. **Insurance Watch:**
   - *Life Insurance Companies Comparison.* Retrieved from Insurance Watch Life Insurance Ratings
   - Compares and rates life insurance companies in Australia.

**International Sources**

5. **NerdWallet:**
   - *Best Life Insurance Companies.* Retrieved from NerdWallet
   - Provides comprehensive ratings for life insurance companies based on consumer experience and financial strength.

6. **Policygenius:**
   - *Life Insurance Reviews and Ratings.* Retrieved from Policygenius
   - Detailed reviews and ratings of life insurance policies.

7. **Money:**
   - *Best Life Insurance Companies of 2024.* Retrieved from Money
   - Rates life insurance companies based on customer satisfaction, financial stability, and policy options.

**Investment and Financial Planning**

8. **Vanguard:**
   - *Vanguard High Growth Fund.* Retrieved from Vanguard Australia
   - Used as an example for growth portfolio investments.

**Superannuation and Retirement**

9. **Australian Taxation Office (ATO):**
   - *First Home Super Saver Scheme (FHSSS).* Retrieved from ATO
   - Details on using superannuation to save for a first home.

10. **SuperGuide:**
    - *Superannuation Fees and Performance.* Retrieved from SuperGuide
    - Information on superannuation fund fees and performance.

**Personal Growth and Development**

11. **Mindfulness-Based Stress Reduction (MBSR):**
    - *Mindfulness-Based Stress Reduction Program.* Retrieved from MBSR
    - Program details used in discussing personal growth strategies for reducing anger and improving patience.

**Tools and Calculators**

12. **MoneySmart:**
    - *Superannuation Calculator.* Retrieved from MoneySmart
    - Useful for calculating superannuation growth and projections.

# Appendix

## Scenario 5.1.

How insurance can help you as a high net worth individual distribute assets evenly.

Here's a simplified example:

### Scenario

Mr. Smith owns a $10 million business, $10 million in other assets and has three children: Alice, Bob, and Charlie. Alice works in the business, while Bob and Charlie do not. Mr. Smith wants to leave the business to Alice but also ensure Bob and Charlie receive equal shares of his estate.

### Strategy

1. **Business to Alice:** Mr. Smith leaves the $10 million business to Alice (assumption - the business was structured properly to be already in a trust easily transferred).

2. **Life Insurance for Bob and Charlie:** Mr. Smith takes out two life insurance policies, each worth $5 million, with Bob and Charlie as beneficiaries.

### Outcome

- **Alice:** Inherits the $10 million business.

- **Bob and Charlie:** Each receive a $5 million life insurance payout, ensuring they get an equal share of the inheritance. They also inherit the other assets, split even between Bob and Charlie.

### Benefits

- **Fair Distribution:** Each child receives an equivalent portion of Mr. Smith's estate.

- **Tax Efficiency:** Life insurance payouts are generally tax-free.

- **Immediate Liquidity:** The insurance proceeds provide instant cash to Bob and Charlie.

Using life insurance to even out inheritance ensures fair distribution, tax benefits, and liquidity, maintaining family harmony and financial stability. This strategy is commonly recommended by estate planning professionals. Only works for high net worth families with concentrated asset positions.

# About the Author

Victor Idoko is a well-regarded and highly qualified financial planner with over 12 years of experience in the financial services industry. He holds a degree in Economics and Accounting, a Master's in Commerce (Finance Major) from The University of Western Australia, a Diploma and Advanced Diploma in Financial Planning, and is a Chartered Financial Analyst (CFA).

Victor's unique upbringing within the Army Barracks of Nigeria, followed by boarding school at a young age, instilled in him a strong sense of independence and a structured approach to life and business. The close relationship and deep respect he holds for his parents and siblings, along with their unwavering support throughout his entrepreneurial journey, have provided him with the confidence to continue growing both personally and professionally. He doesn't take himself too seriously and cares deeply about his work and how he approaches it. Victor is genuine, always open to giving back to the community, and especially passionate about educating children to help them navigate the world more easily. He continuously seeks ways to make an impact not only on his clients but also on his colleagues, family, and friends.

In working with Victor, it becomes clear that he is very goal-oriented, loves numbers, and is both analytical and strategic. His disciplined nature makes him exceptional at what he does, enabling him to add significant value to his clients' individual goals and financial plans. He has assisted me with my own financial goals and future planning as well.

Victor helps his clients gain clarity and direction with their goals, ensuring they avoid mistakes that could jeopardize their hard work or derail their future plans.

Victor and I have also collaborated on delivering clients' financial plans, and I've witnessed firsthand how committed he is to ensuring that these plans are well executed. He is also excellent at holding everyone accountable.

Ultimately, Victor is passionate about living his best, most rewarding, and fulfilling life, which includes continued learning, staying fit, spending time with family, traveling, and running a business that helps clients achieve the same—living a more rewarding and fulfilling life, whatever that might look like for them. This book is yet another example of how he seeks to contribute and make a positive impact on the lives of others.

**Lan Ta**
**Founder & Director of Chic Buyers Agency Buyer's Agent –**
**Helping Australians buy property**
www.chicbuyersagent.com.au

## Author's Note

Writing this book has been an incredible journey. My hope is that the insights and strategies shared within these pages will help you navigate the complexities of financial planning with greater ease and confidence. Remember, financial independence is not just about wealth, but also about the freedom to live life on your own terms. Thank you for allowing me to be a part of your financial journey. Here's to your success and prosperity.

# Author's Financial Planning Google Reviews

**The last 18 Google reviews of the Author's services.**

"I've had the pleasure of working with Victor Idoko from CFV Services as my financial advisor, and I couldn't be more satisfied with the experience. Victor's expertise, professionalism, and dedication to his clients are truly exceptional. He takes the time to understand my financial goals and provides clear, actionable advice tailored to my needs. His proactive approach and thorough explanations have given me confidence in my financial decisions. I highly recommend Victor to anyone looking for a trustworthy and knowledgeable financial advisor."

*Adnan Taveer, Managing Partner Mountain Assets, mountainassets.com.au*

"I highly recommend Victor to anyone seeking a financial adviser that cares. His advice, guidance and knowledge is second to none. He has helped my wife and I get a secure grip on our future by painting a road map that has given us the confidence and excitement to reach our financial goals. Thank you Victor for structuring our finances which will provide us with a stress free retirement whenever we decide to!"

"We engaged Victor from CFV services to help us reach our goals for retirement. Victor spent time understanding our situation and our vision. He then took us through a detailed plan of how we can achieve our goals. What I didn't expect was the level of care and support Victor has provided us with, every step of [the] way, he truly has gone above and beyond. I highly recommend Victor and the team at CFV Services, thanks to them I feel our future is in good hands."

*Wendy, Director at Because You Matter Bespoke Gifting Experience, www.becauseyoumatter.gifts*

"Victor and his team have done an excellent job giving my partner and I visibility over our personal finances and set us on track with achievable budgets that will see us on track to achieve our goals."

*Joanna, Director at Drum Digital, www.drumdigital.com.au*

"We are so grateful to have Victor and the CFV team as our trusted partner in realising and reaching our personal financial goals. After our first year with CFV, it's such peace of mind to have the team with us to ensure our future plans are achievable and on track.

Thank you CFV for helping us prioritise our [financial] security and freedom!"

"Victor and his team have been so helpful with my financial goals and planning for building wealth. Learnt so much and look forward to continuing our working relationship."

"Victor and his team have been instrumental in empowering my wife and I to feel in control of our finances. Each meeting was informative and we always felt like we were making progress. Victor took the time to understand our situation thoroughly and our strategies feel really tailored to us. Really lovely person and experience, would recommend to anyone."

"Victor has been incredibly helpful with not just significantly growing our super but guiding us through our financial health and planning. The results have been fantastic. I would recommend for anyone at any stage of life to make an appointment with Victor."

"Great service! Victor has been super helpful in guiding us through and coaching us with our financial planning. The team is awesome and super helpful. 10 out of 10 service"

"I really enjoyed working with Victor. He provided insightful guidance tailored to our unique financial goals. His expertise helped us navigate complex investment decisions with confidence. Highly recommended for anyone seeking personalised financial planning and wealth management strategies. Exceptional service! Thanks Victor     "

*Bart, Director at Abart Joinery, www.instagram.com/abartjoinery*

"Victor and [team] help us with our financial planning and tax efficiency. We are grateful that they help us avoid making financial blunders."

"What I most like about Victor is his combination of intensity and genuineness. What I mean by that is that he is focused and dedicated in everything that he does, yet his principal focus is centered around how he makes a difference in the lives of the people that he interacts with. You don't get 'half focus' from Victor, when you speak with him, you get 100% of himself. That is rare and incredibly valuable and something I appreciate greatly in both a friend and a colleague. Someone I most definitely want on 'my team' in life."

*Baz, Director at The Social Adviser, www.thesocialadviser.com*

"Victor and the team [are] great and approachable in helping to sort out our funds and cashflow, and we've been enjoying our coaching sessions. I highly recommend them."

"My wife and I engaged Victor and his team in 2022 after putting financial advice off for a long time. My wife and I were always hesitant to let other people have a place in our financial decision making processes and therefore engaging with a financial planner was never something we would consider. Thankfully, some life events occurred which caused us to reconsider our position and we brought on Victor for his advice. To put it simply, we wish we had done it earlier! Victor and his team have been nothing short of exceptional. They are extremely attentive, experienced, readily available and always have our best interests at heart. Thanks Victor and the team!"

"Victor and his team helped us with Cash Flow Management Training that really helped us to sort our accounts … Highly recommend Victor Idoko for any financial planning!"

*Hassan, Director at Healthcare IT Solutions,*
*www.healthcareitsolutions.com.au*

"Competent, professional and [detail]-oriented, all the qualities you would expect from a Financial Planner. But to add to this, Victor displays sound judgement, a cool head and is highly ethical. I would and have recommended Victor to family and friends."

*Danny, Director at Neo Energy (Solar Panels), neoenergy.com.au*

"My wife and I recently started a family and we thought it would be best to plan for our future. We recently sat down with Victor to seek out financial advice to build wealth for our family group. We did some financial modelling with Victor and he was able to provide us with sound investment advice, direction and advise us on different options we could go with. Victor is very knowledgeable and goes the extra mile to explain investment strategies to ensure we understood it all. We have now engaged him [for] wealth management and [can't] wait to live a rewarding life. We definitely recommend Victor!"

*Philip Khao Virtual CFO, Director of Solve Accounting,*
*solveaccounting.com.au/about-us/philip-khao/*

"It has been an absolute pleasure to work with Victor and the team at CFV Services. Victor trusted us to look after his clients and it was amazing to see his care, skill, experience and passion in looking after his clients. Highly recommended for all your financial planning and insurance needs."

*Ury Zhang, Director of Biz Lawyers & Advisory, bizlawyers.com.au*

## Contact Information

You can reach Victor Idoko at:

- Email: victor@cfvadvisory.com.au

- Website: cfvadvisory.com.au

- LinkedIn: Victor Idoko

- Insta: cfvadvisory

- Tiktok: victoridokowlthadv

**Book a Meeting with Victor**

## Future Works/Ideas

Stay tuned for my upcoming book, where we will dive deeper into advanced investment strategies and explore the world of alternative assets especially for family business owners and corporate executives. This next book will provide even more tools and insights to help you continue growing your wealth, balancing health and relationships whilst also securing your financial future. Here's a sneak peek:

"In the ever-evolving world of finance, staying ahead means continuously learning and adapting. In the next book, we'll explore dealing with concentrated positions that often arise for business owners and corporate executives, providing strategies to protect and grow your wealth in these unique circumstances."